Great Prayers of the Bible:
A Guide for Individual or Group Study

50¢

GREAT PRAYERS

OF THE BIBLE

A GUIDE FOR INDIVIDUAL

OR GROUP STUDY

 DAVID L. JENKINS

BROADMAN PRESS
NASHVILLE, TENNESSEE

Unless otherwise stated, all Scripture quotations are from the King James Version of the Bible.
Scripture quotations marked RSV are from the *Revised Standard Version of the Bible,* copyrighted 1946, 1952, © 1971, 1973.
Scripture quotations marked NIV are from HOLY BIBLE: *New International Version,* copyright ©1973, 1978, 1984 by International Bible Society.

Library of Congress Cataloging-in-Publication Data

Jenkins, David L.
   Great Prayers of the Bible: a guide for individual or group study
   / David L. Jenkins.
   p. cm.
   ISBN: 0-8054-1543-2 :
   1. Bible--Prayers. 2. Bible--Study. I. Title.
BS680.P64J46 1990
242' .722'07--dc20

                                                                    89-38435
                                                                    CIP

TO MY CHILDREN Paula Gail Jenkins Mitcham and Christopher Lee Jenkins

CONTENTS

Introduction ———————————— 9
An Introduction to Prayer ———————— 11
1. Prayers of Moses ————————— 15
2. Prayers of Joshua ————————— 23
3. Prayers of Solomon ———————— 34
4. Prayers of Elijah ————————— 45
5. Prayers of Isaiah ————————— 55
6. Prayers of Daniel ————————— 65
7. Prayers of Jonah ————————— 74
8. Prayers of David ————————— 84
9. Prayers of Paul ————————— 98
10. Prayers of Jesus ————————— 112
11. Prayers of James ———————— 126
12. Prayers in the Revelation ————— 141
13. Prayers of the Early Church ——— 155

INTRODUCTION

These *Great Prayers of the Bible* can be adapted for a variety of uses. For example, many people wish to pursue an individual study of the Scriptures by topic. A study of these prayers as they appear successively from Old to New Testaments provides opportunity for such a systematic approach. The specific emphasis of each prayer makes it possible also to choose the prayers at random according to subject.

Because each study is complete within itself, any one of them provides material for a devotional presentation or a one-time study relating to a particular emphasis or interest. Also, many churches promote weekday Bible study groups. A variation from Bible book studies would be to take a topical approach, such as that suggested by the "great prayers" theme. Such a study might be preceded by the general introductory session on prayer and then followed by these individual prayers.

Then, many pastors feel frustration about the midweek service. Traditionally, the Wednesday-night hour has been called "prayer meeting." While some churches may dedicate the time almost exclusively to prayer, most congregations are led in a period of Bible study as a part of that hour. These studies may be used effectively in this setting, also.

There will be detailed study material for each prayer,

which may be adapted to the needs or goals set for the particular session. Then, a brief outline of each section of the study will be included, which the leader may wish to have reproduced on a single sheet of paper for the study participants.

The goal of the study is aimed at the development of a meaningful prayer life among those who constitute the fellowship of believers Christ designated as His church, that He loved, for whom He died.

—David L. Jenkins

An Introduction to Prayer

Each of the prayers presented in this study represents different needs expressed by different persons, often in radically different situations. Except for the prayers of Jesus, they portray the human struggle and spiritual growth of each individual.

In spite of the understandable differences and objectives of the prayers people pray, there are certain general requirements if prayer is to be effective. Thus, prior to considering the prayers included in this study, let's examine the following points of emphasis which will provide a foundation for effective praying.

A Forgiving Spirit (Matt. 6:14)

The attitude we have toward others is an indication of our attitude toward God. True forgiveness is demonstrated when one cares more about the person than about what he has done. Jesus underscored this in the story of the forgiving father (Luke 15), whose concern was for the son returning from the far country and not for what he may have done there.

An unforgiving attitude toward another often amounts to a power play in which the offended person keeps the offender forever in her debt, never letting her forget what she has done. Such harbored feelings of unforgiveness can warp our personalities and reduce us to bitter, obnoxious persons.

Simplicity (Matt. 6:5-6)

Prayer is not a performance but an intimate relationship between an individual and God. The common Jewish posture of prayer in Jesus' day was that of standing. Certainly the physical position we assume when we pray has little bearing on the content or sincerity of our prayers. Apparently, however, the standing position among the Jews sometimes encouraged a hypocritical motive. For when the hours of prayer arrived, some of them enjoyed being on street corners or in the marketplace where people could see and hear them pray.

Jesus' insistence that we enter our closets and pray to God secretly is not a literal requirement for effective prayer. Rather, He was emphasizing the fact that prayer is between the individual and God. It is a simple act of baring our souls before Him as we would share our innermost thoughts and yearnings with our closest friends. We do not pray to impress God but to discover His will for our lives.

Humility and Repentance (Luke 18:10-14)

Jesus' story of the Pharisee and the publican at prayer in the Temple emphasizes humility and repentance; these are the basic attitudes we must have if our prayers are to be heard. The Pharisee's attitude in prayer reflected his self-righteousness. He was a separatist in the most offensive sense of the word, for he considered himself superior to others because of his piety.

The publican was indeed a sinner of the worst kind, as far as his actions against his fellow Jews were concerned. He was a traitor to his country, and in exacting exorbitant taxes from the people, he was guilty of taking that to which he had no right. But he recognized the evil of his ways and humbled himself in repentance before God. In spite of the fact that the Pharisee was morally decent and religiously correct, God commended the publican for genuine humility and repentance, but God condemned the Pharisee for self-righteousness. It is not self-righteousness that provides a basis for prayer, but *God's* righteousness.

Tenacity (Luke 18:1-8)

Jesus' parable of the unjust judge was not intended to apply to prayer in general, as though God is reluctant to respond to our needs. Rather, Jesus sought to teach us that often we must learn to wait in our praying, realizing that there are both design and purpose in God's delays. "Tenacity," or holding on in prayer, reflects our confidence that God's will is going to be accomplished in accord with *His* timetable, and in His own way.

Intensity (Matt. 7:7-11)

In order to pray effectively, we must understand the kind of God to whom we pray. He is a Heavenly Father who longs to give good gifts to His children. Faith is not a blind wish, but actually a response to evidence that God *does* care for His own. *Ask, seek, knock* (v. 7) are verbs that express not only continuous action, but also, their progression suggests a growing awareness of our dependence on God.

The two illustrations Jesus gave concerning a child asking his father for bread and fish were well-known Jewish arguments dealing with the nature of prayer. No doubt Jesus had learned this as a lad in the Nazareth synagogue school. It remains an apt description of our Heavenly Father's sincerity in answering our prayers in relation to our needs.

Confident Expectation (Mark 11:24)

These words of Jesus constitute one of the thrilling prayer promises in the Bible. But it is not to be applied indiscriminately, as a "blank check," with no strings attached. Rather, it presupposes one whose faith is deeply rooted in God's will. Faith that God does all things well is the source of the power of this promise as well as the means of its strength. God's omnipotence is its assurance, and His sovereignty is its only restriction.

Unceasingly (1 Thess. 5:17)

To pray without ceasing does not suggest a continuous act of conscious prayer. Though it does emphasize frequent praying, its intent is to underscore the importance of a prayerful attitude or an awareness that a believer is constantly in the presence of God.

Such an awareness creates a dependence on God that in turn assures one of constant joy, even in the midst of trouble. An uninterrupted awareness of God's closeness to us keeps earthly and heavenly values in balance.

1 PRAYERS OF MOSES

Introduction

Men and women of God who have been entrusted leadership responsibilities understand well the need for prayer. Often a leader of people, at whatever level of life he or she may function, is envied and sometimes misunderstood by those "in the ranks." Though there are great rewards that come to faithful leaders in this life as well as in the next, burdens, pressures, frustrations, and disappointments often are experienced. Those being led are rarely ever aware of the hours a leader must spend in isolation, alone with God, struggling for wisdom and guidance.

Moses was such a leader. From the human perspective, his task was overwhelming. Because he understood the magnitude of the responsibility God had given to him, Moses often was driven to prayer. In this study, we will examine three recorded prayers of Moses which demonstrate the scope of his battles as a leader.

In order to refresh our memory concerning the background of this remarkable man, perhaps a brief review of his life would be helpful. The major events recorded in Scripture that reveal historical facts about Moses give evidence of God's sovereign involvement in his life.

Throughout the long years the descendants of Jacob had

lived in Egypt, many of them had begun to worship the gods of the Egyptians while giving a vague lip service to the true God. Yet there were some, like Amram and Jochebed, Moses' parents who kept their faith in God and cherished their unique relationship to Him as children of Abraham.

Still, considering the pagan atmosphere and the absence of a strong leader after the death of Joseph, the fact that the Hebrew people maintained their faith at all was an amazing evidence of God's sovereignty. He was determined to preserve a people through whom He would carry out His plan of redemption. Though no specific reference to Jochebed and Amram's faith is made in the Exodus account, the writer of Hebrews stated, "By faith Moses, when he was born, was hid three months of his parents, because they saw he was a proper child; and they were not afraid of the king's commandment" (Heb. 11:23).

The involvement of Pharaoh's daughter (Ex. 2:5-9) is further evidence of God's meticulous design in Moses' early life. In spite of the fact she recognized the baby Moses as "one of the Hebrews' children" (v. 6), her heart was captivated by the beautiful and innocent child (v. 2). God took control of her thoughts and plans, seeing to it that the timing of the approach of Moses' sister, Miriam, and her suggestion (v. 7) concerning care of the infant was received favorably.

Though Moses was reared in the affluence and splendor of the palace of Pharaoh and enjoyed all of the benefits of a royal heir, the flame of God's presence and the seal of His ownership remained with Moses. Again, the writer of Hebrews recorded the awakening of Moses' awareness of the destiny of his people, who were being persecuted mercilessly by the new Pharaoh (Heb. 11:23-27).

Before God could use Moses, much mellowing of his personality and mental attitudes was needed. Though his intervention on behalf of the Hebrew slave being treated cruelly by the Egyptian taskmaster was noble and humanly commendable (Ex. 2:11-12), the harshness of his action was not in keeping with God's way. Obviously, Moses ran ahead of God in his desire to become his people's champion and deliverer. The result was forty years spent in the desert of Midian (Ex. 2:15 to 3:20), during which God groomed Moses for the task He had prepared for him.

The story of the burning bush (Ex. 3:2-4) was the first mountain peak in a long range of soaring experiences Moses had with God. This initial battle between Moses' reticence and God's will for his life laid the groundwork for Moses' remarkable courage, which would be displayed ultimately in the face of humanly impossible situations.

Moses' Prayer of Intercession

Exodus 32:9-32

Moses' relationship with his people is an example of a pastor's heart. He came to experience early in his association with his fellow Israelites the agony of intercessory prayer.

God's anger (vv. 9-10).—While Moses was on the mountain receiving the Ten Commandments from God, the people decided that he was not going to return and lapsed into their past inclinations toward idolatry. God's conversation with Moses regarding this gross infidelity of the people shows the unique relationship that existed between them. God's suggestion that Moses "let [Him] alone" (v. 10) and not interfere with His determination to destroy the sinful people was an obvious test of Moses' faith. On the basis of God's covenant with Abraham, Isaac, and Jacob, He probably would not have destroyed all of the people. God wanted to hear Moses' intercession for the people.

Moses' intercession (vv. 11-13).—In spite of their sinful behavior, Moses loved the people deeply. In the tradition of a true mediator, Moses first asked God why His anger burned against *His* people, whom *He* had brought up out of Egypt "with great power, and with a mighty hand" (v. 11). If God carried out His threat to destroy the people, the remarkable display of His power on their behalf would have been wasted. The Egyptians would be convinced that the God of the Hebrews had led them into the desert to kill them. The Egyptians would win after all. Then Moses concluded with his strongest argument. Not only were the lives of God's own people at stake, along with His name among the Egyptians, but also His very trustworthiness in light of His oath (Gen. 22:16; Heb. 6:13,17), the promise of His covenant, and His name (Ex. 3:15).

God's response (v. 14).—In the face of Moses' earnest prayer, God relented. As yet, of course, the people had not repented of their sin, and thus God's forgiveness had not been secured (v. 30). Moses' intercession had only averted God's destruction of the people.

On behalf of the people, Moses confessed the great sin they had committed. Moses stood in the gap for his people, and with deep emotion he made a magnificent offer. Though the people did not deserve the love Moses displayed toward them, still he offered to have his name removed "out of thy book which thou hast written" (v. 32). The implication is that Moses was willing to perish in the place of his people, if only they might be forgiven and saved from God's wrath. God's reply to Moses was, in essence, that He punishes only those who sin against Him. The people would be spared, but they would suffer the consequences for their sin.

Moses' Prayer of Despondency

Numbers 11:4-17

Moses was capable of reaching spiritual heights in his relationship with God, but he also was subject to periods of depression and despondency.

The occasion (vv. 4-6).—In spite of the fact God had fed the people with manna which was not only delectable to the taste but contained all the nutrients needed for their physical health and strength, the record states that "the children of Israel also wept again, and said, Who shall give us flesh to eat?" (v. 4). In the midst of their complaining, their mouths began to water for the fish, cucumbers,melons, leeks, onions, and garlic they had enjoyed in Egypt (v. 5).

God's plan questioned (vv. 10 15). Moses' prayer to God reveals much concerning his coping ability at this point in the wilderness journey. No doubt he was physically exhausted and worn out by the frequent complaining and murmuring of the people. Obviously, he was spiritually discouraged. His first statement to God implied that this reaction of the people was a personal attack upon him, permitted by God. Moses felt that, for some reason, he had fallen into divine disfavor. He asked God to kill him at once. He was ready to throw up his hands and abandon the project.

Moses' dilemma understood (vv. 16-17).—God did not reprimand Moses for his expression of discouragement. Instead, He gave Moses a remedy for the immediate problem, amounting to a distribution of the crushing responsibilities that rested on Moses' shoulders. Moses was instructed to appoint seventy men to share his administrative load. God would anoint them with the same Spirit with which He had endowed Moses.

Moses' Prayer for God's Presence

Exodus 33:9-13

God's people in Old Testament times did not enjoy the presence of the indwelling Holy Spirit as believers do today as a result of the Spirit's advent at Pentecost. Instead, God would come upon them in the presence of His Spirit and empower them for specific ministries and assignments. This accounts for their frequent periods of questionable conduct and feelings of estrangement and alienation from God during the interim periods when they were not engaged directly in divinely-appointed service.

God's presence in the cloud (v. 9).—God had instructed Moses to set up the tabernacle (the tent of worship) outside the camp of the people. While the people watched from the doors of their tents, Moses entered the tabernacle, and God came down in "the cloudy pillar" (v. 9) and talked with Moses. The pathos and longing of Moses' heart are reflected in his prayer. He admitted that he did not know the way, and would be powerless to lead the people without divine guidance.

Recognizing a need for guidance (vv. 12-13).—Moses felt often his need for God's reassuring presence with him. On this particular occasion, immediately following the incident involving the golden calf (Ex. 32), God had indicated to Moses that He would not "go up in the midst" of the people (Ex. 33:3) as He had done in the past, probably referring to His presence manifested in the cloud and pillar of fire. Moses deplored the idea of not having God's presence with him and with the people.

He chose to suffer with his people (32:32).—Though Moses often experienced disappointment and frustration because of the attitudes and actions of the people, he never sought to disassociate himself from them. They were his people, and he was a part of them. If they perished, he would perish. Moses knew that an effective leader must be willing to identify with his people at all times, bearing their burdens and suffering their pain.

Application

The first of the three prayers of Moses reviewed in this chapter deals with intercessory praying. Following this prayer, the worship leader may wish to ask for prayers of intercession for specific needs in the lives of individuals. True intercessory prayer involves a deep concern and burden for others. It is more than the superficial discharging of a duty in praying for someone and then promptly forgetting it. Intercessory prayer is a lingering prayer experience during which you suffer vicariously with the person or persons for whom you are praying.

A similar procedure may follow the second prayer dealing with Moses' despondency. Many people today suffer depression for various reasons. The group may be asked to pray silently for someone whom they know is experiencing depression because of either temporary or irreversible problems.

In the third prayer, Moses invoked God's presence and guidance. The final prayer period could be directed toward a need for God's presence in one's daily life experiences.

(The outlines that follow the "application" portion of each chapter can be reproduced on a half sheet of 8½-by-11-inch paper for distribution to the study participants.)

Outline: The Great Prayers of Moses

Introduction

In the providence of God, men and women are raised up from time to time and are used as instruments in the working out of His plans and purposes in providing redemption for sinful people. Such a person was Moses, who was destined to be the founder of the Israelite nation, its deliverer, lawgiver, historian, and prophet.

Moses' Prayer of Intercession: Exodus 32:9-32

1. God's anger (vv. 9-10)
2. Moses' intercession (vv. 11-13)
3. God's response (v. 14)

Moses' Prayer of Despondency: Numbers 11:4-17

1. The occasion (vv. 4-6)
2. God's plan questioned (vv. 10-15)
3. Moses' dilemma understood (vv. 16-17)

Moses' Prayer for God's Presence: Exodus 33:9-13

1. God's presence in the cloud (v. 9)
2. Recognizing a need for guidance (vv. 12-13)
3. Moses' choice to identify with his people (32:32)

2 PRAYERS OF JOSHUA

Introduction

Why God chooses certain men and women to lead His people or to perform unusual or heroic tasks for His glory can be ascribed only to His sovereignty. For sometimes those whom He selects seem quite unpromising at first, or at least they seem poorly equipped for leadership roles. But then, as the divine plan and purpose unfold, so do the characters and strengths of these persons.

The Scriptures do not state why God chose Joshua for the great responsibility of succeeding Moses as leader of the Hebrew people. However, certain facts about Joshua's early life and developing strengths can help us understand God's selection. Apparently, Joshua was born in Egypt, although nothing is recorded about his parents. His grandfather, Elishama, is mentioned as having been a leader of the tribe of Ephraim during the wilderness journey (Num. 1:10; 1 Chron. 7:27). Joshua is first mentioned in Exodus 17:9, where Moses instructed him to choose men to fight against the Amalekites who were harassing the Hebrews. This would indicate, of course, that Joshua had already proved his military skills to the satisfaction of Moses. We know also that Joshua and Caleb were the only adult Israelites who came out of Egypt and survived the 40 years of wandering who were allowed to enter the Promised Land.

An outstanding characteristic of Joshua was his undaunted courage. He demonstrated this when he and eleven other Hebrew men returned from spying out the fortified cities of southern Canaan. Joshua and Caleb were alone in their contention that, in spite of the size of the enemy, the Lord was capable of giving them the victory (Num. 14:9). Joshua also was a man of unqualified obedience both to the Lord and to Moses, his superior.

From the early chapters of the book that bears his name, we can discover that Joshua was prepared by God to fulfill his role in the divine plan through the experiences he had during the forty years' journey through the wilderness between Egypt and Canaan. Joshua also had the opportunity of serving under Moses, the aged statesman of the Israelites, and noting the way Moses handled crises, frustrations, distress, and victory. Then, of course, God revealed Himself and His plans for the future of His people to Joshua, and promised that His presence and power would be with Joshua (Josh. 1:1-9).

A Prayer God Could Not Answer

Joshua 7:7-9

The taste of victory is always sweet. Yet human nature being what it is, a continued diet of victory and conquest can cause people to become haughty and overconfident in their own strength and prowess. Such was the case with one of the Israelites. With his fellow soldiers, Achan had savored repeated victory and success in their encounters with the Canaanites.

In a subtle and sinister way, haughtiness and an inordinate amount of self-confidence had settled like a dark mantle over the people. Such a state is followed by carelessness in one's attention to obeying God's will and keeping His law. In this instance, an entire army was affected because of the disobedience of one person. Often the fellowship of a whole congregation of believers can be interrupted because of the disobedience and sin of one member of the body.

The Hebrew word translated "trespass" (7:1) is a technical term referring to the misappropriation of property that was considered sacred (see Lev. 5:15). In this instance, the trespass had to do with the "accursed thing," suggesting that Achan was dealing with a clearly revealed prohibition that God had given. So the stage was set for one of the darkest hours in the early history of the Israelites in Canaan.

The source of defeat (vv. 1-5,10-12).—The power of God had been demonstrated again and again in the victories of the Israelites over the Canaanites. The fall of Jericho no doubt had practically paralyzed the people of Canaan with fear and awe before the advancing Israelites. Thus, in preparation for the next phase of the campaign, Joshua dispatched men from Jericho to the city of Ai. Generally associated with the ancient site of et-Tell, Ai was in the central hill country of Palestine, near Bethel where Abraham had lived upon his arrival in Canaan (Gen. 12:8).

After having searched the area surrounding Ai, Joshua's spies returned with a glowing report of the possibility of victory. They suggested that only 2000 or 3000 men would be needed to conquer the city since the people there were "but few" (v. 3). As he had done before, Joshua took the advice of his men and organized about 3000 men to attack Ai. Yet when the battle began, Joshua's men were surprised to find that the men of Ai were superior and had the upper hand from the beginning. Joshua's fighting men panicked and fled toward the rocky cliffs that led down to the Jordan Valley (v. 5). Thirty-six Israelites were killed, and the rest of the army reached Gilgal completely humiliated by this totally unexpected defeat.

The record states that "the hearts of the people melted, and became as water" (v. 5). Oddly, a similar descriptive phrase was used earlier to describe the attitude of the Canaanites when they were about to be defeated (2:11; 5:1).

The prayer of agony (vv. 6-9).—Upon hearing the news, Joshua was devastated. In the typical Hebrew expression of grief, Joshua tore his clothing and fell prostrate on the earth in great disappointment and sorrow. As an added expression of their deep sorrow and humiliation, Joshua and the elders of Israel put dust on their heads (see also Gen. 37:34; 1 Sam. 4:12; 2 Sam. 1:2; 13:31).

From the human standpoint, Joshua's first reaction at hearing of this unbelievable defeat was understandable. Before the conquest of Jericho, God had assured Joshua of victory. Then, in a most unique and miraculous way, Jericho had fallen, and God had thus confirmed His promise to Joshua. Thus we can imagine the feeling of despair and disillusionment that must have come upon Joshua when he heard that his crack fighting troops—accustomed to seeing the enemy flee before them in fear—had been soundly defeated. God had promised victory and had allowed His people to relish its sweet taste. And now, *this*! Surely Joshua thought *This just cannot happen to us*!

In Joshua's first statement to God, he raised a question that, in essence, was raised by the unbelieving and murmuring Israelites during the wilderness journey (see Ex. 16:2-3; Num. 14:2-4). Joshua was concerned about the destiny of his people, of course. In a display of almost petulant anger, he asked God why He had allowed His people to enter Canaan, if they were going to be destroyed by their enemies. But he also expressed concern about what effect this defeat would have among the pagan Canaanites in regard to the name of

God (v. 9). How this defeat must have hurt Joshua's *pride*! He must have wondered if God would intervene to save His *own* name, if not the name of His people.

The way God answered (7:10f.).—Joshua learned that there are times when prayer is out of order. He had "the cart before the horse." He was asking for God to intervene and save the day before he admitted the reason for the fiasco in the beginning. Sin had to be confessed and forsaken.

A Prayer that Produced a Miracle

Joshua 10:12-15

We have a saying in Western society that "a man's word is his bond." Perhaps, however, in a day when people tend to do what is right in their own eyes, believing that "the end justifies the means," such a concept of truth and integrity is no longer a major consideration. In the ancient Near East, a formal oath or covenant was extremely important and binding. For example, as a result of a shrewd ploy on the part of the Gibeonites, the Israelites were deceived into making a covenant with them that the Gibeonites would not be destroyed, but they would be allowed to live in peace among the Israelites. God had told Joshua to rid Canaan completely of the pagan Canaanites. The Gibeonites had misled Joshua into believing they had come from a far country, seeking peace with the Israelites. Instead of making the issue a matter of prayer, Joshua and his people accepted the Gibeonites and vowed to protect them. They soon learned, however, the mistake they had made.

The result of the covenant with the Gibeonites (vv. 1-6).— This covenant resulted, then, in the inhabitants of the important city of Gibeon making peace with Joshua and the Israelites. The pagan king of Jerusalem could see a potential tragedy in all of this. Other strategic cities in the vicinity of Jerusalem might do the same thing and thus leave Jerusalem vulnerable to attack. So Adoni-zedek, king of Jerusalem, sought the cooperation of five other kings in Canaan and, with their combined forces, set out to punish the Gibeonites for making a covenant with Israel. As soon as the Gibeonites heard of Adoni-zedek's plot, they sent word to Joshua at Gilgal, reminding him of the agreement he had with the city of Gibeon and requesting protection in fulfillment of that agreement.

The response of Joshua (vv. 6-8).—Realizing that he *did* have an obligation to protect the city under the conditions of the covenant, Joshua responded quickly to the call. By the time he had gathered his forces together, it was afternoon. They began their march from Gilgal, fortified with assurance from the Lord God that He would be with them in battle. Even though the relationship with the Gibeonites was initiated in the midst of deception, coupled with the possibility that Joshua shared in the guilt by not seeking God's will before making the covenant with them, God said to Joshua, "Fear them not: for I have delivered them into thine hand; there shall not a man of them stand before thee" (v. 8).

The miracle of nature (vv. 10-11).—Not only is the battle that followed one of the most unusual in Israel's history, it is also the strangest battle in *all* recorded history. Joshua's men had traveled all night from Gilgal to reach Gibeon. They were exhausted from the long journey. The battle began in the morning, the Israelites prevailed against the Amorite coalition, and wholesale destruction resulted. The enemy army was fleeing in disarray when God sent a terrifying hailstorm that, miraculously, affected only the enemy and not the Israelites! This was not a natural hailstorm, for the stones fell only on the enemy and not on Joshua's armies.

As the battle wore on, Joshua soon realized that his army would not be able to win the battle before nightfall. If they suspended the fighting during the nighttime, then the enemy would have opportunity to rest and regroup. The weary Israelites would have difficulty fighting them again the next morning. All of this became clear to Joshua. So, while the enemy was scattered and frustrated because of the hailstorm, Joshua decided that the time was right to capitalize on the situation.

Joshua's strange prayer and God's answer (vv. 12-13).— Seeing that his army needed just a little more light in which to complete their battle victoriously against the Amorites, Joshua prayed, "Sun, stand thou still upon Gibeon; and thou, Moon, in the Valley of Ajalon."

The text of Joshua's prayer, according to the biblical record, came from the book of Jasher, which seems to have been a collection of ancient heroic songs, probably compiled about the time of David. The poetical form and composition of Joshua's prayer would indicate that it was part of a song. These odes in praise of certain heroes of the theocracy also contained historical facts about their achievements. The book is referred to again in 2 Samuel 1:18, relating to an elegy written about Saul and Jonathan. It is generally believed that the book was lost during the time of the Babylonian captivity. Jasher means "the upright," or "the righteous man."

Just how God brought this miracle to pass, we do not know, nor is it important at this point. The Scriptures state that there was enough light for Joshua and his army to prevail, for "the sun stood still in the midst of heaven, and hasted not to go down about a whole day" (v. 13). The five kings and their armies fled to Makkedah, about twenty miles from Gibeon. The following day the kings were discovered in a cave near Makkedah. Joshua commanded that they be taken from the caves so that the captains of the Israelites could put their feet on the necks of these kings. This was a symbolic act indicating the complete defeat of an enemy. After this, the kings were slain (v. 26). The wonder of this miracle was noted in the statement, "There was no day like that before it or after it, that the Lord harkened unto the voice of a man: for the Lord fought for Israel" (v. 14).

Application

These two prayers of Joshua present an excellent study in contrasts. Up until chapter 7 of the Book of Joshua, the Israelites had been basking in the glow of victory. They had crossed the Jordan without opposition from the Canaanites, observed the Passover at Gilgal, and took Jericho without the loss of a single warrior. No doubt Joshua himself felt that nothing but success lay ahead for his people.

However, temptation often comes when we are enjoying the exuberance of success. Without doubt the people had begun to feel, whether consciously or not, that they were invincible. Probably their thoughts of God and their dependence on Him had been pushed farther and farther into the backs of their minds. God did not plan for them to suffer defeat at Ai. His desire certainly was that they experience unbroken victory in the conquest of Canaan.

Likewise God desires that His children live in constant victory over sin. In fact, He makes it possible for us to *do* this, as long as we live in the power of His Spirit. But He does not make it impossible for Christians *not* to sin. Defeat need not happen, but it may. The reasons for the Israelite defeat at Ai are the same as the reasons why Christians often are defeated. First, there was self-confidence. They were in the flush of victory. There is no moment as dangerous in the life of a Christian than the moment the believer emerges victoriously from some battle or some deep trouble.

The second reason for Israel's failure at Ai was, apparently, a lack of prayer. There is no evidence in the opening verses of chapter 7 that Joshua prayed before laying his plans for the conquest of Ai. If he had prayed, God could have revealed to Joshua that there was "sin in the camp" in the disobedience of Achan, and the Israelites would never have experienced their humiliating defeat. When one prays in the midst of victory, there will be no need to plead in a time of defeat. To pray for deliverance in the midst of defeat really is useless. How did God respond to Joshua's prayer? "Get thee up; wherefore liest thou thus upon thy face?" (7:10).

A third reason for Israel's failure at Ai was disobedience. One man, Achan, had sinned, but the whole army was defeated. The Israelites were a nation, but God was dealing with them as a corporate body through whom He intended to carry out His ultimate plan for providing redemption. So God's verdict was *not* "Achan hath sinned," but "Israel hath sinned" (v. 11). When one member of a fellowship of believers sins, the effect permeates the whole body. God's verdict is: My people have sinned. The point is that no individual Christian can disobey God's law without affecting others, thus lowering the spiritual temperature of one's church family. The ultimate victory of the whole community depends on the victorious life of every individual member.

In Joshua's second prayer (ch. 10) we saw evidence of God's total concern about the affairs of His people, particularly when they are engaged with that which relates to His will and purpose. Not all prayers that we pray automatically produce immediate and visible results in the nature of what we expect. Nor does God always perform instant miracles for us when we pray. Sometimes it is His will that we answer our own prayers, and He chooses to give us wisdom and guidance in the way to do it. Yet other times, as in the incident of Joshua's battle against the Amorite kings, miraculous intervention is God's method of meeting the needs of His people.

Most Christians, at one time or another in their lives, experience answers to prayer that are nothing less than miraculous. The factors and influences that come together to change a situation, for example, cannot be attributed to coincidence. Or a physical healing transpires that defies the predictions and breaks all the rules of medical science. In order for God's will to be accomplished in a particular situation, He may choose to circumvent normal circumstances, or even His own natural laws. Such was the nature of God's answer to Joshua's prayer about this battle.

What were the "side effects" of this miracle? The account states that "none [of Israel's enemies] moved his tongue against any of the children of Israel" (10:21). In other words, Israel gained respect in the eyes of the enemy because they saw evidence of God's power manifested on behalf of His people. When God's people in *any* age show evidence of their faith in His power to answer prayer and to provide for their total needs, the world will take notice. A fellowship of believers should be uncompromising in their testimony and convictions, courageous in their faith, and holy in the way they live. Their lives should be such that their strongest critics can find no legitimate reasons to question their sincerity.

Outline: The Prayers of Joshua

Introduction

The sovereignty of God was evident in the choice of Joshua to succeed Moses as the leader of the Hebrew people. Not only was Joshua groomed personally by Moses, but also Joshua was able to observe at close range the prayer life of that great giant of God. Yet Joshua's spiritual pilgrimage, like that of Moses and every other child of God, was not without its weaknesses and difficult times.

A Prayer God Could Not Answer: Joshua 7:7-9

1. The source of defeat
2. The prayer of agony
3. The way God answered

A Prayer that Produced a Miracle: Joshua 10:12-15

1. The result of the covenant with the Gibeonites
2. The response of Joshua
3. The miracle of nature
4. Joshua's strange prayer and God's answer

3 PRAYERS OF SOLOMON

Introduction

The outstanding men and women of the Bible each had distinguishing characteristics that were unique to them that God used to advance His program on earth. For example, we think of Solomon generally in terms of his divinely bestowed wisdom. And indeed, Solomon revealed evidence of remarkable skills in military conquest, foreign policy and diplomacy, economic and building expansion at home, and, at the beginning of his reign, a spirit of rare devotion and humility before God. Yet the end of Solomon's life was marked by sins often produced by the decadence accompanying great wealth and prosperity.

The two prayers of Solomon that we will focus on in this study give insight into the heart and soul of a man who recognized his and his people's ultimate dependence upon God in order to receive His blessings and assurance of His divine guidance and help. Solomon understood the importance of setting the proper priorities in his life and in the affairs of his kingdom.

The two Books of Kings contain several powerful and impressive prayers prayed by kings and prophets alike. We must remember that these prayers were prayed during a period in the development of God's people when His grace had not yet been revealed in Jesus Christ. Consequently, the concept of God as a personal and approachable Deity was rare and, obviously, a revelation of God's Spirit. Thus, in these prayers, we catch glimpses of God's progressive work of revealing Himself to His people. With Jesus came the full revelation of God. Jesus continues to reveal the unfathomable facets of His nature and being to those who make themselves available to the revealing ministry of His Spirit.

A Prayer for Wisdom

1 Kings 3:5-9

Solomon's prayer for wisdom at the beginning of his reign as king of Israel reveals that already he had a perceptive understanding of the task that lay before him. In spite of the wealth and royal splendor Solomon had inherited from his father David, he anticipated something of the awesome responsibility involved in ruling a people who often were rebellious and difficult to lead.

The nature of Solomon's monarchy.—In the opening verses of 1 Kings 3, we discover evidences of Solomon's shrewdness as a leader in the area of foreign policy. In fact, the method Solomon used principally to establish relationships with foreign kings and nations probably contributed to his downfall. Here, he had married the daughter of Pharaoh; and, through the years of his reign, he continued to make these marital alliances with other foreign monarchies.

Then, we also see evidence here that the Israelites had taken over the shrines of the Canaanites and were using them as places to worship Yahweh and to offer sacrifices to Him. The author of 1 Kings explained this practice by stating that "the people sacrificed in high places, because there was no house built unto the name of the Lord, until those days" (v. 2). Apparently, there was a major shrine at Gibeon, about seven miles northwest of Jerusalem. For some reason not revealed, Solomon went there to worship on this occasion rather than to offer his sacrifices at the tabernacle in Jerusalem. Archaeological excavations have revealed that a prominent hilltop shrine near Gibeon proper was probably the leading country shrine in the area. Our Scripture passage refers to it as "the great high place" (v. 4). This may explain the reason Solomon chose to go there to worship God on this occasion.

Solomon's inherent desire.—The author also noted that "Solomon loved the Lord" (v. 3). The Hebrew word for *love*, *ahav*, denotes a moral concern and commitment rather than mere affection. It does not reflect the depth of intelligent love revealed in the Greek word *agape*. The concept of God as a personal and approachable Being was probably still vague in the minds of these Old Testament people.

Solomon's prayer at Gibeon was spontaneous in that it was not a planned prayer, nor even a prayer in the ordinary sense of the word. Solomon offered the petition to God in the midst of a vision that came to him. In this nighttime vision, God said to Solomon, "Ask what I shall give thee" (v. 5). Solomon responded first by referring to the many instances in which God had delivered his father David from trouble and supplied his needs. Solomon pointed out that David had been trustworthy and honorable before God, which Solomon saw as grounds for David's deserving God's goodness expressed toward him. God had blessed David further by giving him a son to succeed him to the throne. No greater disfavor could come upon a king than not to have a son to continue the dynasty and rule.

In the midst of that encounter with God, Solomon immediately became aware of his inadequacy to rule "a great people, that cannot be numbered nor counted for multitude" (v. 8). Solomon saw himself as "a little child" before God, even though he had to have been a married adult at the time he became king. After forty years of rule he was said to have had a son age forty-one (1 Kings 11:42; 14:21). Solomon was saying to God that he was a child in his understanding of how to govern so great a people.

God's response.—Though God's offer to Solomon seems to have been a blank check with no conditions or restrictions, we can be sure that in His omniscience, God knew Solomon's heart and anticipated His request. Often people say that Solomon is to be commended for requesting what he did, for he could have *asked* for greater wealth and power among the nations of the world. He may well have asked for those things, but it is doubtful that God would have granted such selfish requests had they been uppermost in Solomon's thinking.

Instead, Solomon asked God for "an understanding heart to judge thy people, that I may discern between good and bad" (v. 9). In that moment we can imagine that the full weight of the role Solomon was to play as king of Israel rested heavily upon his shoulders. He was aware that Israel was a chosen people of God, and a holy destiny was involved in their existence.

God's answer was marvelous in its scope. The gift of wisdom God would give to Solomon would be of such magnitude "that there was none like thee before thee, neither after thee shall any arise like unto thee" (v. 12). Then, because Solomon's priorities *were* correct, God announced further that He would give Solomon "both riches, and honor" that would elevate him above his royal peers (v. 13). Furthermore, God concluded His conversation with Solomon by assuring him that if he would "walk in my ways, to keep my statutes and my commandments, as thy father David did walk, then I will lengthen thy days" (v. 14).

In all fairness, we must note that as the years passed the young, idealistic Solomon became more and more interested in building a lavish capital city. His extensive building projects all but enslaved his people, and his continued compromises with foreign countries and with their religions weakened the moral and spiritual fiber of his own people. At Solomon's death, Israel as a kingdom was so weak that it could no longer hold together. The result was a divided kingdom. Thus, in the life of Solomon we find both an ideal to be followed and a warning to be heeded.

Solomon's Dedicatory Prayer

2 Chronicles 5—6

Introduction

A great moment had arrived in the history of Israel, as well as in the personal life of King Solomon. The king had brought to reality the dream of his father David—building a house of worship and sacrifice for God. King David had despaired that, while he lived in a palace of cedar, God was still being worshiped in a tent. So he began an extensive program of planning and gathering materials and money for the project.

Because of David's life as a warrior and mighty man of battle, God did not allow him to complete the temple. That privilege was granted to Solomon, David's son and successor to Israel's throne. Solomon had carried out his father's plans for the building, and now it stood completed in shining, regal splendor.

The temple building.—After seven years of building, the

fabulous edifice was completed (2 Chron. 5:1-2). Solomon might well have basked in the glory of what had been accomplished, for it was he who had painstakingly overseen the project, taking care that the most minute details were attended to. Nothing was spared which could give strength, beauty, and perfection to the temple. Solomon saw to it that nothing inferior should go into this magnificent building that would house the very presence of God.

The furnishings of the building and its courtyard were in place: the altar of brass, the ten lavers, the ten candelabra, the ten tables for the shewbread, and all the vessels to be used in the temple rituals. Though it was far beyond Solomon's comprehension in that ancient day, these furnishings were gloriously symbolic of God's ultimate plan for humankind's salvation. The altar represented redemption while the lavers spoke of sanctification or perpetual cleansing. The candelabra pointed to Christ as the Light of the world, whereas the tables bearing the loaves of bread typified Him as the Bread of life.

In the holy of holies, the elaborately sculpted golden cherubims were in place, and underneath and between their outstretched wings was the mercy seat and the ark of the covenant. The golden cherubims represented heaven's approval upon God's condescension to come to earth in the Person of His Son to bear the sins of the world on the cross.

Solomon's address to the people.—Apparently, an elaborate program had been planned for the dedication of the temple. For 2 Chronicles 5:11-14 describes the activities and music program designed by the priests and musicians. "Cymbals psalteries and harps" (v. 12) are mentioned, along with the "trumpets . . . and instruments of music" (v. 13). But no sooner had the priests uttered their call to worship than the temple was filled with a cloud (v. 13), the visible representation of the presence of God. This is a good illustration of the fact that Spirit-led planning for worship is good and acceptable. However, there may be times when our best planning can interfere with God's desire to do things His way. No doubt the dedicatory program that had been planned for the new temple was beautiful and would have been very impressive. But God interrupted their plans in order to do things *His* way.

Solomon recognized God's glory and told the people about his father David's experience with God concerning plans for the temple (2 Chron. 6:1-11). Solomon's genuine humility was obvious in this experience. The typical Eastern king gave feasts and planned events in order to call attention to himself and to exalt *his* majesty. An indication of Solomon's honesty is revealed particularly in this statement he made to the people: "The Lord therefore hath performed his word that he hath spoken: for I am risen up in the room of David my father, and am set on the throne of Israel, as the Lord promised, and have built the house for the name of the Lord God of Israel" (v. 10).

Solomon's prayer of dedication.—Second Chronicles 6:12-42 contains Solomon's actual prayer of dedication for the temple. Solomon took pains to impress upon the people the seriousness of the occasion. He had a brass scaffold built before the great altar of sacrifice on which he knelt and prayed, with hands outstretched toward heaven. First, Solomon gave the glory to God for the completion of the temple. Then he honored his father David, reminding the people through his prayer that plans for the fabulous temple began in the heart and mind of David.

Then, with a remarkable flash of understanding regarding the universal aspect of God's relationship to humankind, Solomon included this statement in his prayer: "But will God in very deed dwell with men on the earth? behold, heaven and the heaven of heavens cannot contain thee; how much less this house which I have built!" (v. 18). In an era when the Hebrew people considered Yahweh as mostly concerned with them, Solomon recognized the omnipresence of God, and that, actually, no "house" could contain a God who desired to dwell in the entire earth.

In verses 19-21, Solomon prayed for himself and his people. He asked that God would hear his prayer, and that His "eyes may be open upon this house day and night" (v. 20). Because God had not yet come to dwell *within* His people (as He did on the Day of Pentecost in the Person of the Holy Spirit), they needed visible reminders of His presence among them.

Another evidence of Solomon's depth of understanding about God's means of dealing with His people was his reference to forgiveness (v. 21). In essence, Solomon was saying that the people must accompany their praying with repentance, and thus receive God's forgiveness. This formula for effective praying is equally imperative for God's people in *any* generation. We, too, must see that our sins are confessed and forgiven before our praying can be effective.

In verses 22-39, Solomon prayed for future worshipers who would come to the temple. He recognized the tendency of the people to sin and to disobey God's commandments, noting that God's judgment upon them would be an automatic response. Solomon implored God to forgive and restore them when they repented of their sins. He mentioned not only personal and individual sins the people might commit but also corporate sins that could result in drought and pestilence upon the land and invasion by enemy peoples. Solomon also prayed for the "stranger" (v. 32), who would come to worship in the temple, that *his* prayers might be answered. By this, they would "know that this house which I have built is called by thy name" (v. 33). Perhaps a measure of prophetic insight was present in Solomon's prayer when he prayed that if the sins of his people should result in their being carried away captive into an alien land, God would hear their prayers of repentance and restore them to their own land.

Solomon concluded his prayer with a moving benediction (vv. 40-42), in which he reiterated an earlier petition that God's attention be focused continually upon the temple and the prayers that would be offered there. He asked God to enter "into thy resting place, thou, and the ark of thy strength" (v. 41). He also prayed that God would honor the ministry of the priests who, by virtue of their office, would intercede before Him for the salvation of the people. If these prayers were answered, then indeed the people would "rejoice in goodness" (v. 41).

Application

The lesson in Solomon's prayer for wisdom to rule God's people is a simple and obvious one. In fact, the structure is dramatic in its simplicity: God offers, and Solomon responds to the offer. God answers, and Solomon worships in genuine gratitude for God's blessing. God's offer was: "Ask what I shall give thee." God's giving responded to Solomon's asking, insofar as it corresponded with God's intention to do what was best for Solomon and for the Israelite people. Solomon "loved the Lord," that meant he was committed to pleasing God to the best of his ability. Thus, his asking would be in the context of his devotion to God.

Our petitionary prayers reveal what kind of persons we are. Solomon's request for an understanding heart showed what kind of leader he desperately wanted to be. As noted earlier in this study of Solomon's prayers, he did not reach the potential that God surely desired for him. Nor did he rise to the spiritual heights he might have reached. We have difficulty reconciling Solomon, the vengeful opportunist and political pragmatist, with the humble, receptive petitioner seeking divine wisdom. Perhaps we should remember that every person seeking to follow God's will is a walking civil war, constantly battling those opposing forces and temptations that would pull one down from the heights where one walks with God.

The theme to be pursued in the study of Solomon's prayer of dedication upon the completion of the temple is obviously God's insistence that He receive glory and honor above any accomplishments His people might achieve, however outstanding and noteworthy they may be. The importance of praise in relation to one's concept of God must be central, preceding and preempting all other facets of prayer.

The study may be lengthened somewhat by extending the Bible material to include God's answer to Solomon's prayer (2 Chron. 7:1-5) and the unique way in which God manifested His glory, not only to Solomon and to the priests but to all of the people. Then, God's personal appearance to Solomon in the night, whether in a dream or in a vision, contained the great promise of revival and restoration for God's repenting people (Chron. 7:12-22).

In the period of prayer to follow the Bible study, emphasis might be placed first on specific reasons to praise God for His sovereign power and for His benevolence demonstrated in various ways toward His people. Ask the people to recall particular ways in which God has revealed His goodness to them, personally, as well as to the church in general. If time permits, brief, personal testimonies could be included here.

Outline: The Prayers of Solomon

Introduction

These two prayers of Solomon present the great king of Israel at his greatest spiritual stature. The first prayer laid the foundation for the caliber of leadership that would characterize the early part of his reign. The second prayer revealed Solomon's unselfish desire to dedicate the magnificent temple to the glory of the God for whom he had built it.

A Prayer for Wisdom: 1 Kings 3:5-9

1. The nature of Solomon's monarchy
2. Solomon's inherent desire
3. God's response

A Prayer of Dedication: 2 Chronicles 5—6

1. The temple building
2. Solomon's address to the people
3. Solomon's prayer of dedication

4 PRAYERS OF ELIJAH

Introduction

In the light of the Scriptures, a prophet was one who was divinely inspired to communicate God's will to His people and to disclose the future to them. The Hebrew word most often used for *prophet, nabi,* means "a declarer or announcer." The prophets of Israel played a unique role in the spiritual development of God's people. They were outstanding among biblical characters because they were able to understand and interpret what was happening around them in the light of God's character and purpose. In a sense, they became the guardians of the nation's conscience. The recorded prayers of these prophets reflect their sensitivity to God's will. There were instances when they did not accept God's intention for the people or for themselves without question. Sometimes they would protest vigorously, but they always acquiesced to God's will. These struggles are evident as one studies the prayer lives of the prophets. Certainly they kept their eyes open toward God. But they also talked with Him. At times it seemed that they talked to Him almost as much as He spoke to them.

The role of prophecy among God's people developed somewhat progressively. As Jesus described the kingdom of God, there was first the blade, then the ear, and, finally, the full

corn in the ear (Mark 4:28). In the beginning, an enthusiastic group of men known as "the sons of the prophets" appeared (1 Sam. 10:5). They were followed by a second stage
of prophets who were men of action such as Nathan, Elijah,
and Elisha. They moved through the land as God's represen-
tatives. Their ministry was one of correction, encourage-
ment, and warning both to the kings and the people. God's
Word was spoken directly through them. Sometimes they
are called "preliterary prophets" because they did not write
down their prophecies. All that we know of them comes
from biblical stories written about their experiences.

The third group, sometimes called the literary prophets
because they wrote down their messages, prophesied from
the eighth century down through the Exile of the Jews in
Babylon. Amos, Hosea, Isaiah, Jeremiah, Ezekiel, and others belong to this group. They did not say as much about
what was going to happen in the future as they did about
what God was doing currently.

Elijah, two of whose prayers we will examine in this chapter, came from Tishbeh in Gilead. Gilead, a mountainous
region east of the Jordan River extending from the Sea of
Galilee to the upper end of the Dead Sea, was about sixty
miles long and twenty miles wide. It was noted for its beautiful scenery, forested hills, and its many herds of cattle.
The tribes of Reuben and Gad asked Moses for permission to
claim this territory because of their need for pastureland
for their herds. Beyond the fact that Elijah was a native of
Gilead and apparently a member of one of the two tribes of
Israel that settled there, we know nothing more about this
colorful prophet's personal history.

Elijah lived in a day when the worship of Yahweh was
being threatened by the local religions of the Canaanites.
Baal was the chief god worshiped among the people of Canaan. The particular responsibility of this god was supposed

to be the care of crops. Since the area of the Northern Kingdom of Israel where Elijah ministered was an agricultural country, Baal's influence was great. Baal worship practices were very immoral, and those who participated in it indulged in gross sensuality. Some of the Israelites openly worshiped Baal; others wanted to worship Yahweh in the manner that Baal was worshiped. Such a blasphemous approach to the worship of the true God incensed Elijah, and he opposed the spread of Baalism with all of his strength. As a result of the sins of the people, Elijah had declared to King Ahab that rain and dew would be withheld from the land (17:1). The result was a great famine that lasted three years (18:1).

A Prayer of Persistence

1 Kings 18:41-46

Elijah often was quite dramatic in his unique ministry among Israel. The incident that precipitated the first of two prayers we will study grew out of a contest Elijah proposed on Mount Carmel between Yahweh and the prophets of Baal. The time had come to "draw the line" once and for all.

Elijah's challenge to the people (vv. 20-21).—Elijah had challenged the people, "How long halt ye between two opinions? if the Lord be God, follow him: but if Baal, then follow him." The response to his challenge was: "The people answered him not a word." The arrangements Elijah made by which to bring this matter to a head were simple. They consisted of two altars with a bullock upon each and two prayers for fire to consume the offerings. The God who answered by fire would be the true God.

The contest between God and Baal (vv. 22-38).—Four hundred and fifty priests of Baal prayed and leaped about the altar all day, finally cutting themselves in the hope that the sight of blood would bring response from Baal. When evening came, it was Elijah's turn. He called the people near. To make the test conclusive so that no one would doubt the power of Yahweh, Elijah had twelve jars of water poured upon the offering, the wood, and the altar. A God who could start a fire in the midst of that would be a true God indeed! Elijah's prayer was simple and to the point (vv. 36-37). The fire fell, and the demonstration of God's power was so complete that not only the offering and the wood were consumed, but also the stones of the altar and the very dust around it were burned up.

The response of the people and of Elijah (vv. 39-41).—The people were convinced anew of the power of Yahweh and fell on their faces in repentance. There was no way the people could mistake the evidence they had seen demonstrated before their eyes. They declared, "The Lord, he is the God; the Lord, he is the God" (v. 39). Then Elijah announced to King Ahab that already there was a "sound of abundance of rain" (v. 41), signifying that the devastating drought was about to end. It remained then for Elijah to exercise *his* faith in prayer.

The exercise of a true faith (vv. 42-46).—After Elijah instructed the king to go to the palace to "eat and drink" in celebration of the end of the famine and the coming of the refreshing and life-saving rains, Elijah and his servant "went up to the top of Carmel" (v. 42). Elijah may have had a special place there where he communed with God. Though Elijah, by faith, had heard the sound of an "abundance of rain" in his heart, there was yet no visible sign of rain. In a demonstration of humility and submission to God, Elijah sat on the ground with his head between his knees. The words of the prophet's prayer to God are not recorded, although he probably prayed that God would complete the work He began when the fire fell from heaven to consume the sacrifice. The repentance of the people and their public recognition of God as Lord of their lives would be the triggering response to the lifting of the famine judgment.

Another implication in this story emerges with the involvement of Elijah's servant in this prayer experience. Elijah told the servant to go and "look toward the sea" (v. 43). The servant returned, no doubt disturbed because of the news he must deliver to his master. He told Elijah that he saw nothing. The sky was clear. Undisturbed by the news, Elijah told the servant, "Go again" (v. 43). Six times the servant went to the brow of the hill, only to bring word to his master that he saw nothing. Finally, when the servant returned the seventh time, he reported, possibly with some hesitation, that a tiny wisp of a cloud, hardly the size of a man's hand, had arisen out of the sea.

That was all Elijah needed. As far as he was concerned, the answer was complete. He sent his servant to tell Ahab to prepare his chariot and leave at once for Jezreel, which may have been the location of the king's summer palace. After the three years' drought, the soil in the valley of Jezreel likely was covered with a deep layer of dust, with all vegetation long since gone. The drenching rains that were coming would turn the dust into a bed of mud, and the wheels of Ahab's chariot would stick fast in it.

Sure enough, the heavens turned black with clouds and wind, and the rains came. The biblical historian recorded that Elijah "girded up his loins, and ran before Ahab to the entrance of Jezreel" (v. 46). Perhaps Elijah did that for several reasons. First, he proved his own humility, recognizing himself only as God's spokesman and seeking no praise for himself. Second, his presence before the king would be a reminder of what God had done in the contest with the prophets of Baal, and in the rescinding of the famine judgment.

Elijah's presence might also have strengthened Ahab, at least temporarily, to withstand the temptations of his wife, Jezebel, who took advantage of Ahab's weaknesses to carry out her ungodly causes as a priestess of Baal.

A Prayer of Futility

1 Kings 19:1-8

From the heights of glory and victory for God and His prophet, Elijah, in chapter 18, we plunge quickly into the deep valley of despair in chapter 19. Elijah, having come so soon from the "victory run" from Mount Carmel to Jezreel, sat now in a crumpled heap beneath a juniper tree and prayed for God to take away his life.

Before we criticize Elijah too harshly for his actions, we must remember that two other biblical greats reacted in a similar fashion under stress. Moses, the great lawgiver and prince of God, prayed to die in exasperation over the rebellious conduct of the Hebrew people whom he had been called to lead from Egyptian slavery to the Promised Land (Num. 11:15). Then Jonah, in a fit of petulant anger, told God that he preferred death rather than witness the repentance and salvation of the pagan Ninevites to whom he had preached (Jonah 4:1-9).

The wrath of Jezebel (vv. 1-2).—Elijah probably intended to carry his crusade to overthrow Baal worship in Israel to Jezreel. Fired by the victory at Mount Carmel, he likely felt that nothing could stand in the way of a sweeping spiritual victory that would restore the nation to God's favor. But when King Ahab told Jezebel, his pagan queen, what had happened on Mount Carmel and how the prophets of Baal had been slain by Elijah, she reacted with violent anger. Jezebel had been a Phoenician Baal worshiper when Ahab took her to be his wife as part of a political alliance with her father, Ethbaal, king of Tyre and Sidon. The slaying of the prophets of Baal incensed her to the point of seeking retaliation against Elijah. She sent a messenger to Elijah to inform him that by the same time the next day she would have him slain in the manner that he had put the Baal prophets to death. Her words probably were intended as a threat, for, doubtlessly, she feared the people who were now enthusiastic supporters of Elijah. Had she truly intended to kill Elijah, she would have dispatched assassins to do the job instead of sending a messenger to threaten him. She simply wanted to frighten Elijah into leaving the area.

The response of Elijah (vv. 3-4).—Upon receiving the threatening message, Elijah did exactly what Jezebel wanted him to do. He left the country! He and his servant fled south to Beer-sheba in Judah where he apparently dismissed his servant. Elijah probably felt that his ministry was over, having failed to finish his work by ridding Jezreel of Baal worship and destroying the influence of the evil Queen Jezebel. The fact that Elijah left the kingdom of Israel and went to the Southern Kingdom of Judah may also have been his way of saying that he was finished with his people, Israel. He was, in a sense, shaking the dust off his feet, as far as his ministry there was concerned. Jeremiah reached a low point in ministry when he, too, expressed a desire to leave his people for a lodging place in the wilderness (Jer. 9:2). In his despondency, Elijah left Beer-sheba and went a day's journey farther into the desert to pour his heart out to God and yield himself up to Him. His plaintive cry was, "It is enough; now, O Lord, take away my life; for I am not better than my fathers" (v. 4). His forefathers were in their graves. They were at rest and no longer faced the rigors and disappointments of life. Elijah was ready to die, for he considered himself no better than they.

The answer from God (vv. 5-8).—Sleep came to the distraught Elijah as a soothing relief for his troubled soul. Like a tender and understanding parent, the Lord God dispatched an angel to comfort Elijah. In his distress, he probably had not eaten. Great sorrow and anguish often diminish one's physical appetite. The angel touched Elijah to awaken him, and then told him to eat. Elijah did so, promptly lay down again, and went back to sleep. How long Elijah was permitted to sleep this time, we are not told. But the angel touched him a second time and again suggested that he rise and eat. This time, a reason was given: "because the journey is too great for thee" (v. 7). The trip that lay ahead for Elijah would require all the strength that food could provide. In fact that heaven-provided food made it possible for Elijah to travel for forty days and nights before he reached the mountain of God (v. 8). So Elijah's prayer to die was a futile prayer, for God still had work for His prophet to do. And God intended for him to do it.

Application

These two prayers prayed by the prophet Elijah provide an interesting study in contrast. In the first prayer, we see the prophet Elijah at one of the highest moments of his life. He was God's spokesman and instrument in the bringing about of a great spiritual victory and revival among the sinful and disobedient Israelites. But in the second prayer, which followed closely after the first one, we find Elijah at perhaps the lowest point in his ministry. He was begging to quit, even to die.

This study provides opportunity to examine one's reaction in times of victory as well as in times of defeat. In the first prayer, we see the ideal reaction of one whose faith in God is secure and unshakable. Elijah had done as God had instructed him about the contest with the Baal prophets on

Mount Carmel. He had dismissed King Ahab with the promise that the rains were coming to relieve the three-year drought. But still there was no sign of rain! Elijah did not give up. He sent his servant to look for the cloud seven times. We must indeed pray, but then often that is not enough. The exhortation is "pray, and not to faint" (Luke 18:1; Eph. 5:18; Col. 4:2). Elijah persisted in prayer until the answer came. There are reasons for God's delays in answering our prayers. We may not learn the reasons in this life, but we can be sure that He who knows the end from the beginning of our lives will do what is best for us within the realm of His will.

Elijah's prayer to die was indeed a pitiful prayer. But it bears out the truth that Satan often attacks us when we are basking in the sunlight of victory. For then we tend to become more self-confident than God-reliant. Worn out in body and mind, Elijah became vulnerable to fear. His ministry had not been a popular one with the royalty of Israel. It had been costly and exhausting. He was often misunderstood, causing him to experience an overwhelming sense of loneliness. But the visit of the angel demonstrated to Elijah that our God is a tender and understanding God.

Outline: The Prayers of Elijah

Introduction

These two prayers of Elijah give an excellent insight to the extremes to which God's people can go in the exercise and realization of their faith. They provide an opportunity to review our spiritual pilgrimages in the light of times of victory and of despair, and our reactions toward those contrasting experiences.

A Prayer of Persistence: 1 Kings 18:41-46

1. Elijah's challenge to the people
2. The contest between God and Baal
3. The response of the people and of Elijah
4. The exercise of a true faith

A Prayer of Futility: 1 Kings 19:1-8

1. The wrath of Jezebel
2. The response of Elijah
3. The answer from God

5 PRAYERS OF ISAIAH

Introduction

As with Elijah, very little is known about the personal history of Isaiah. The opening verse of the Book of Isaiah informs us that Amoz was his father, but there is no record of the tribe of which he was a member. Most Bible scholars believe Isaiah lived in Jerusalem, near the Temple, based on the information in chapter 6. He is further thought to have married a prophetess by whom he had a son named Maher-shalal-hash-baz (8:3). Another son, Shear-jashub, is also mentioned (7:3).

Isaiah's prophetic ministry spanned the reigns of four of Judah's kings: Uzziah, Jotham, Ahaz, and Hezekiah. During the reigns of Uzziah and Jotham, Isaiah confronted the people with their sins and urged them to repent, but they did not respond. He then was forced to announce coming judgment and banishment for his people. The second period of Isaiah's ministry extended through the rule of Ahaz, and the final phase lasted from the time Hezekiah ascended Judah's throne through the fifteenth year of his reign. From that time, Isaiah seems to have played no active role in public affairs. He lived until the beginning of Manasseh's reign when, according to tradition, he was martyred. The statement in Hebrews 11:37 regarding some being "sawn asunder" is thought to be an allusion to the manner in which Isaiah was executed.

Isaiah was one of the most brilliant of the writing prophets. Second Chronicles 26:22 and 32:32 refer to biographies of Kings Uzziah and Hezekiah that Isaiah wrote; these were inserted in the lost annals of Judah and Israel. Isaiah is best known for his incomparable prophetical descriptions of the person and offices of the Messiah.

Isaiah appears to have been highly recognized in Jerusalem. When King Hezekiah sent a deputation to him, he sent his highest officers and the elders of the priests (2 Kings 19:2). Isaiah may have been the leader of the prophetic order, holding in Jerusalem the same rank that Elisha held in the schools of the prophets in Israel. He lived to see his prophecies fulfilled regarding the Babylonian Exile, the victories of the Persian Empire's King Cyrus, and the deliverance of the Jews. In fact, according to the Jewish historian Josephus, Cyrus was prompted to free the Jews because of the prophecies of Isaiah concerning himself.

Recorded prayers do not appear often in the writings of the prophets. The reason is not because these men of prophetic insight and faith did not pray. Rather, their works were made up largely of sermons and oracles they delivered to the people. The average preacher's collection of sermons would contain few prayers, although much prayer saturated the preparation and writing of his sermons. So it was with the prophets.

The first of two prayers recorded by Isaiah that we will examine is extremely personal. It concerns the transforming vision that came to him, inaugurating his prophetic mission. The second prayer reflects Isaiah's delight in recognizing that God's peace is available to all who will trust in Him, and will wait for His will and purpose to be revealed.

A Prayer Admitting Sin

Isaiah 6:1-13

This stirring account of Isaiah's transforming call seems out of place at chapter 6. Normally, we would expect Isaiah's book of prophecies to *begin* with the account of his encounter with God. This is not uncommon, however, for we find a similar arrangement in the Book of Amos (7:14-15). If Isaiah's prophecies are arranged according to a plan in keeping with his overall message, then the location of chapter 6 is in proper sequence.

Whatever one's opinion on the matter, this chapter stands apart as a unique record of how God's call came to a man, and how a prophet was born. The encounter was engraved so indelibly on Isaiah's mind that every detail was vividly clear. It was recorded both as a monologue and a first-person narrative. But surrounding it all is evidence of the same basic experiences that come to every person who, as a sinner, encounters a holy and righteous God.

In the presence of God (vv. 1-4).—King Uzziah's long reign was over, and the king had died the humiliating death of a leper. At the age of sixteen Uzziah had been the people's choice to succeed his father, Amaziah, to Judah's throne. During his reign of more than fifty years, Uzziah had strengthened the walls of Jerusalem and had been a strong supporter of agriculture. He never deserted the worship of the true God, and he succeeded in bringing a level of prosperity to the kingdom it had not known since the time of King Solomon. As was often the case, however, Uzziah's popularity and prosperity produced an ego problem. He determined to burn incense on the altar of God but was opposed by the high priest, Azariah, and eighty others. Uzziah was enraged at their opposition, and when he determined to approach the altar with his censer, he was stricken with leprosy.

No doubt this was a traumatic time for the prophet Isaiah. This remarkable vision came to him in the Temple of God. Whether Isaiah was physically in the Jerusalem Temple, or was transported there in a visionary experience, is not clear. Isaiah had been accustomed to the royal splendor of King Uzziah. But due to the king's sin and resulting death as a leper, Isaiah saw that earthly glory can come to a rapid and tragic conclusion. But not so with the glory of God. When Isaiah stated that he "saw also the Lord," he did not mean that he saw Yahweh, the essence of God. For the Scriptures state conclusively, "No man hath seen God at any time" (John 1:18). Rather, Isaiah saw the manifestations of the *glory* of God. His *train*, the skirts of His robes, filled the Temple. Hovering above the throne surrounded by God's glory were *seraphim*, which means literally "burners." These heavenly creatures burned with love to God and zeal for His glory. The presence of these celestial beings made a profound impression on Isaiah. He noted that they had six wings. Four were used to cover themselves in humility before God, and two were for flight.

We have no idea how many seraphim Isaiah saw hovering over God's throne. He heard them shouting to each other, "Holy, holy, holy, is the Lord of hosts: the whole earth is full of his glory" (v. 3). By definition, God is "holy," but He reveals His holiness by His decisions and acts. God's glory could not be contained in the Temple, but it filled the entire earth. The sound of praise reverberated with such force through the Temple that Isaiah saw the doorposts moving, and the smoke of incense from the golden altar swirled and filled the house of God.

The purging of Isaiah's sin (vv. 5-7).—Probably Isaiah's

first inclination was to join in the exuberant praise, but, suddenly, he realized that he could not. He uttered an awesome word in those ancient times. "Woe is me!" (v. 5), he cried. *Woe* is a word of judgment or impending doom. Isaiah recognized that his very existence was threatened because he was sinful. In chapter 5 he had pronounced six woes upon others because of their sin. Now he pronounced a seventh woe upon himself. He was "undone," lost, ruined, because of his sin nature. Because of sin, Isaiah considered his lips, and the lips of his people, unclean and thus not fit to praise God. At this point, Isaiah may have been astounded that he had been allowed to *see* the glory of God and still live. How presumptuous to think that he dare *speak*! Isaiah's prayer of confession revealed his awareness of his sinful state, and it made him a candidate for God's cleansing touch. Again God sent a seraph to perform the purging rite that made it possible for Isaiah to speak.

The call to share (vv. 8-10).—The interference of sin that had prevented Isaiah from hearing God speak was cleared. His heart was clean before God. He could hear the divine call now with no hindrance or distortion. When God asked whom He might send forth with the message of hope and salvation, Isaiah was ready to respond. Not only was his heart clean, but it was filled with a testimony to share. He placed himself at God's disposal with no reservations. Then God gave him a message to proclaim. He was to be merely the channel through whom God would speak His word to the people.

The duration of the call (vv. 11-13).—There was probably a tone of lament in Isaiah's plaintive question: "How long?" He knew the decadent state of the kingdom and the spiritual condition of his people. He may even have suspected that they would not listen, much less take to heart the word of judgment Isaiah must proclaim to them. But Isaiah must prophesy the word of the Lord faithfully until the end. Then he would have delivered his soul and discharged his responsibility before God.

A Prayer for Peace

Isaiah 26:3-12,20-21

The prophet Isaiah ministered during the period of Judah's decline that culminated in the eventual captivity of the people. Isaiah's ministry, like that of many of the prophets in the Old Testament era, dealt chiefly with rebuke, exhortation, and warning of judgment to come. He longed to see his people enjoy the peace of God. Though Isaiah cherished his own personal relationship with God and no doubt rejoiced often in the memory of his encounter with God recorded in the sixth chapter of his prophecy, he must have spent many days in deep sadness and grief for Judah. If only they would do that which would ensure the peace of God within and among them!

A formula for peace (vv. 3-4).—"Thou wilt keep him in perfect peace, whose mind is stayed on thee: because he trusteth in thee" (v. 3). The focus of Old Testament Scripture is more often on the nation of Israel as a whole than upon individual Israelites. Yet there are these rare jewels where the emphasis is shifted momentarily to the individual. The thought here is clear. The nation that comes to cherish its faith in God is made up of individuals who have placed their trust in the Lord.

Their kings had made unholy alliances with pagan nations. They had married the daughters of alien kings and had brought them and their strange gods into the land that flowed with milk and honey. The result was inevitable. The sinful customs and pagan practices of these foreign people had both adulterated and demoralized God's people. Their spiritual security had been destroyed, and their trust in the true God who had given them their land was threatened by their illicit relationships with pagan deities. We can almost hear the plaintive cry of the prophet as he poured out his soul to them: "Trust ye in the Lord for ever: for in the Lord Jehovah is everlasting strength" (v. 4). The formula for peace of heart and soul has not changed. It was and is forever the same: trust in the Lord Jehovah, and in Him only.

A prophet's heart laid bare (vv. 9-10).—Isaiah's exposure to the irresponsible attitude of his people toward their sin and disobedience toward God led him to search his own heart "in the night" (v. 9). When he lay down to sleep, there was no rest, for he found within him an insatiable desire for God. He could see divine judgment coming, and Isaiah's heart went out in compassion toward his sinful people. God had been gracious to the people, but they had ignored Him. It seemed inevitable that God's judgments must be unleashed upon His sinful people before they would "learn righteousness" (v. 9). But alas! Sin had so blinded the people that they did not even recognize the favor of the Lord that had been shown them. With evidences of His blessings all around them, the people still were not able to see them.

A time to remember (vv. 12-15).—In these words, Isaiah reminds us of the heartbroken prophet Hosea (Hos. 14). God had dealt harshly with Israel's enemies. He had lovingly and tenderly poured out His blessings upon His own people. It was as if Isaiah had suddenly realized the contrast between the way God had dealt with Israel and with the nations that had opposed His people. This awareness moved Isaiah to confess the great unworthiness of those who had received such blessings from God. And all of these blessings came in spite of the fact Israel had given her allegiance at times to "other lords."

The light of hope (vv. 20-21).—In spite of the terrible judgment that must come because of sin, there will be another time when God's wrath will have passed by. But during the period of suffering, the people were to find peace in the assurance that this time of judgment upon them would come to an end in God's time. Even while they were in Babylonian captivity as punishment for their sins, they were to keep themselves separate and apart from the surrounding pagan influences of their captors. Even in those awesome circumstances, they could find the peace of God in the knowledge of His promised deliverance.

Application

Of all the prayers of Isaiah recorded or alluded to throughout his prophecy, the two listed in this study probably reveal more clearly the character and personality of the prophet than any of the others. The first prayer in which Isaiah confessed his sin (6:1-13) is a masterful pattern with which to trace the progression of conviction of sin through personal awareness to confession and cleansing. All of these facets of spiritual transformation were experienced by Isaiah. The study of this humble prayer Isaiah prayed when he "saw also the Lord . . . high and lifted up" provides opportunity to see the universality of what is involved in a conversion experience. Though the details will vary with the individual, the time, and the place, the path toward spiritual reality never varies. A good exercise for everyone who studies Isaiah's prayer in which Isaiah admitted his sin would be to trace one's own spiritual pilgrimage from self to the Savior, from darkness into light.

The second of Isaiah's prayers in this study, the prayer for peace, reveals the spiritual maturity of the prophet at this point in his ministry. He was fully aware of divine judgment awaiting his people. They were on a collision course with disaster. But, in spite of their rebellion and disobedience, they were still God's people; and He would deal with them as sons and daughters. They would experience the anguish of separation from God in Babylonian captivity. They would be divorced from their land and from their beloved Temple. They would be surrounded by pagan influences. But if they would put their trust in God and stay their minds (v. 3) on Him and not on the influences and circumstances surrounding them, they would experience His peace. And the peace of God would keep them secure and confident in the midst of their dilemma.

God's people often find themselves in circumstances that threaten their sense of spiritual security and peace. Sometimes these circumstances are of their own making, and other times they are not. But whichever is the case, the solution to the dilemma is the same. If the people trust in God and concentrate on His goodness both in the past and in the present, confessing their sins and asking for God's mercy, the peace of God will surround them and keep them secure in His loving care.

Outline: The Prayers of Isaiah

Introduction

The two prayers of Isaiah in this study provide a vivid portrait of this prince of the prophets. We see him at the moment of his spiritual transformation, and later we see his compassionate concern that his people experience the peace of God in the midst of their dilemma.

A Prayer Admitting Sin: Isaiah 6:1-13

1. In the presence of God (vv. 1-4)
2. The purging of Isaiah's sin (vv. 5-7)
3. The call to share (vv. 8-10)
4. The duration of the call (vv. 11-13)

A Prayer for Peace: Isaiah 26:3-12,20-21

1. A formula for peace (vv. 3-4)
2. A prophet's heart laid bare (vv. 9-10)
3. A time to remember (vv. 12-15)
4. The light of hope (vv. 20-21)

6 PRAYERS OF DANIEL

Introduction

No record exists of the prophet Daniel's family background, although he seems to have been of royal or at least noble descent (Dan. 1:3). Indications also show that he was a brilliant young man, richly endowed with both physical and mental attributes (1:4). He was taken to Babylon along with three other Hebrew youth of rank at the first deportation of the people of Judah.

The Babylonian authorities quickly recognized the high caliber of these young men and pressed them into service at Babylon's royal court. Daniel gained the favor of his Babylonian guardian, Melzar, who allowed Daniel to waive the royal edict that he and his companions be fed the rich food from the king's table. Most of the food was considered unclean by the Hebrew people. God blessed these young men because of their determination to remain pure and true to the teachings of their faith.

Daniel quickly rose to prominence in Babylonian circles because of his divine gift to interpret dreams. His popularity in Babylon aroused the jealousy of his pagan colleagues whose conspiracy resulted in Daniel's being thrown in the lion's den. God miraculously saved him from the beasts, and he was elevated to the highest post of honor in the Babylonian empire (ch. 6). Daniel's ministry covered the time of the Jews' Exile in Babylon, although he lived to see his people return to their homeland. His age did not allow him to return with them, and there is no biblical record of his last years and death. Daniel was conspicuous for his purity and knowledge even during his youth. Daniel's exemplary character is mentioned in Ezekiel's prophecies (14:14,20; 28:3).

The Book of Daniel is one of the most important prophetic books in the Old Testament. Many see it as an introduction to New Testament prophecy dealing with the "times of the Gentiles" (Luke 21:24), the second coming of Christ, the resurrection, and the judgments. Both Daniel and Ezekiel, contemporary Jewish prophets in Babylon, knew how to cope with adversity through prayer. Through the pages of his prophecy, Daniel revealed his dependence upon communication with God through prayer. He knew that because of the unique and difficult circumstances in which he lived, he must rely upon God for wisdom and grace. Daniel maintained an altar of prayer that he visited daily (6:10).

A Prayer for Understanding

Daniel 2:14-23

Arioch, the commander of Nebuchadnezzar's guard, was about to carry out the king's command to kill the wise men of his court because they had been unable to reveal the king's dream he could not remember or interpret it for him. Daniel and his three companions were among the "wise men" and were also slated to die. Daniel asked Arioch why the king had issued such a harsh decree. When Arioch told Daniel about the dream, Daniel asked to be allowed to have an audience with the king. The request was granted, and Daniel was successful in securing a stay of execution long enough to consider the matter and report back to the king concerning the dream.

The wisdom of Daniel (vv. 14-18).—Daniel knew at once what he must do. An interpreter of dreams—even Joseph—had never been required to reconstruct a dream *and* interpret it. But Daniel's faith was such that he believed God could do this unprecedented thing and bring glory to Himself. Daniel laid the matter before his three friends, and they obviously entered into a prayer covenant to pray for God to resolve this matter.

Daniel could have prayed privately, for he was the one who must appear before the king, tell him the dream, and then interpret it. But Daniel knew the value of corporate prayer, too. So he returned home and placed the issue before his three friends. He urged them to join with him in earnest prayer that God would be merciful and reveal to him the king's dream, and then make it possible for him to explain its mystery to Nebuchadnezzar. Daniel did not presume to demand that God come to their rescue by suggesting that their goodness warranted divine favor. And not to be minimized was the fact that if Daniel did *not* successfully reveal and interpret the king's dream, they all faced certain death!

The answer from God (v. 19).—"Then was the secret revealed unto Daniel in a night vision" (v. 19).—Just how God chose to relate Nebuchadnezzar's dream to Daniel, along with its interpretation, is not clear. Some interpreters think Daniel may have fallen asleep and dreamed the same dream the king had dreamed. Others believe a messenger from God appeared to Daniel in a vision and related to him the contents of the dream and its meaning. How Daniel received the answer to his prayer is not important. The fact that God heard and answered the prayers of Daniel and his friends is what really mattered.

The gratitude of Daniel (vv. 19b-23).—Daniel did not first approach Nebuchadnezzar and relate the dream he had been given in his night vision just to be sure that it was the correct dream. It never occurred to Daniel to doubt that what God had revealed to him was indeed the king's dream. His faith in God was pure and unshakable. So before he went to the king, he "blessed the God of heaven" (v. 19). His faith was such that he thanked God in advance for answering his prayer. Already Daniel had seen many evidences of God's miracle power and intervention in his life. Why should he doubt now?

Daniel's expression of thanksgiving was in the form of a hymn consisting of four stanzas (vv. 20-23). It was a hymn of praise to God for His power and wisdom. In His wisdom, God had revealed to Daniel deep, secret things which human beings, within themselves, could not know. God is light. Darkness, which hides truth, cannot exist in His presence.

A Prayer Confessing the People's Sin

Daniel 9:1-19

Daniel 9 is one of the great chapters in the Bible that underscores the nature of an effective prayer of confession. Here we see the spiritual depth and sensitivity of Daniel as he bared his own soul before God and interceded with agony and compassion for his people.

Daniel—a man of spiritual insight (vv. 1-3).—Daniel was a student of history as well as an inspired prophet of God. When King Cyrus finally invaded Mesopotamia and attacked Babylon itself, his heart must have rejoiced to see prophecy being fulfilled before his very eyes. For Isaiah had prophesied years before that God would give Cyrus success (Isa. 45:1-4,13). History was moving forward under the sovereign control of God. The time was right for Daniel to intercede with God for the people that God would cause Cyrus to let the Jews return to their Promised Land, and complete the fulfillment of the prophecy.

How a true believer intercedes (vv. 4-6).—Daniel did not enter God's presence brashly or overly self-confident. Rather, he had preceded his prayer time with serious spiritual preparation. He had fasted, mourned, and clothed himself with sackcloth (v. 3). Daniel knew that he could not approach God on the basis of any goodness on the part of his people. Because of their sins, they had forfeited any claim they might have to God's mercy and grace. They had embraced the heathen gods of their pagan captors and had become an immoral people. Because they had blatantly broken the covenant God had made with them, the people deserved the destruction of their cities and property and the loss of their freedom and their homeland.

Daniel had only one approach from which to petition God's mercy. He prayed that God would glorify Himself by showing the riches of His mercy and grace in pardoning and restoring His guilty people upon their repentance. Thus would the thrilling prophecies of Jeremiah be fulfilled (Chs. 25,29).

The painful admission of guilt (vv. 7-11a).—One of the worst things that could happen to the people was to be humiliated in the eyes of the pagan nations surrounding them. In the days of Moses it was said of them, "For you are a people holy to the Lord your God. The Lord your God has chosen you out of all the peoples on the face of the earth to be his people, his treasured possession" (Deut. 7:6, NIV). God had promised them victory over their enemies as long as they remained faithful to Him, and the nations would respect them. But now all of that had changed. From the time King Josiah died in battle at Megiddo (609 B.C.), the nation had suffered defeat at the hands of the Egyptians and the

Babylonians. Instead of being held in high regard by their pagan neighbors, they were objects of scorn. Their land had been laid waste, and many of their people had been either killed or exiled as slaves. They were mocked because of their claim to know the one true God. Worst of all was their shameful ingratitude toward their God, whose pardon and mercy they refused to accept.

Recognizing the justice of God (vv. 11b-14).—Daniel felt that it was more important for God to maintain His integrity and abide by His moral law than for His sinful people to escape the consequences of their wrongdoing. The people of Judah had been instructed well in the truth of God. They knew His laws, and the consequences for breaking them that had been spelled out so plainly to them. If they could defy God's laws and engage in idolatry and immorality without being punished, why should anyone serve Him, or obey His laws? All that had happened to the Jews—the fall of their Holy City, the destruction of their temple, their Exile to a foreign land—actually had vindicated the holiness and righteousness of their God, and it had demonstrated to the world what kind of God He is. Daniel did not attempt to defend his sinful people, nor to excuse them for their shameful behavior. Without qualification he admitted their guilt.

A plea for forgiveness and restoration (vv. 15-19).—Again Daniel, like Moses in his prayer of intercession after the golden calf incident (Ex. 32:12-13), appealed on the basis of God's own honor and glory. The worst thing about what had happened to the people was that if their temple and their land remained in ruins, the surrounding pagans would have all the more reason to conclude that the God of Israel was not superior to the gods of the Babylonians.

God had promised pardon and restoration if the people would repent of their sins. Daniel did not make his appeal on the basis of the righteousness of the people or that they were God's chosen ones. Instead, Daniel threw himself and his people upon the mercy of God.

Application

The two prayers of Daniel considered in this study provide an excellent view of the character and faith of this young prophet of God. Daniel was intellectually brilliant, attested by the fact the Babylonian captors recognized that he would be a valuable asset to the royal court of their empire. But Daniel was also deeply devoted to his God, and he demonstrated his faith consistently.

In Daniel's prayer for understanding in regard to the interpretation of Nebuchadnezzar's dream, two facets of his faith were evident. First, he believed firmly that God could perform the humanly impossible. The demand of the king was not only that his wise men interpret the dream that had troubled him, but they had to relate the dream to him since he could not recall it! The king's wise men and magicians could not do it, of course, and the angry king decreed that all of the wise men in the kingdom be killed, which included Daniel and his three companions. Instead of giving way to panic—or at the other extreme, accepting fate with a stoical attitude of resignation—Daniel placed the matter before God. The only thing to be done was to identify the king's dream and interpret it. Often our reaction to a serious crisis is first to panic, and then to resign ourselves to what we believe will be terrible consequences. Sometimes unpleasant or even tragic consequences do develop, but when we place our faith in God, He gives "coping ability" to deal with even the most devastating situation. Other times, when we exercise our faith as Daniel did, God sees fit to reverse a seemingly hopeless situation. This, of course, is what happened in Daniel's case.

The second facet of Daniel's faith that was noteworthy in

this particular prayer experience was his decision to involve his three friends in intercession for God's intervention. There are times when the nature of our need calls for private prayer. We must do as Jesus suggested, "enter into [our] closet" and intercede, one on one, with our God (Matt. 6:6). Other times the support of fellow believers in prayer is valuable. God's answers do not come any faster or more willingly as a result of "bombardment" on the part of many prayers. The effect of corporate prayer is that the faith of the individuals praying usually is strengthened in the knowledge that others share the same concern.

The second prayer in which Daniel confessed his and his people's sin before God is a tender and winsome portrait of the humility of God's prophet. Though it is unlikely that Daniel was guilty of the sins of idolatry and immorality that plagued his people, still he recognized his weaknesses, and he identified with his people with no reservations.

Sometimes we are inclined to feel a bit self-righteous when we see a professing Christian engage in some activity or attitude contrary to the teachings of God's Word. Perhaps it is an open sin of immorality or dishonesty. *We* would never be guilty of such a moral infraction against God's laws! And yet we are victims of other sins, hidden sins and sins of attitude, that grieve God's Spirit. Daniel freely included himself with his people in his prayer of confession.

Another noteworthy element in this prayer was Daniel's obvious concern for the reputation of his God among the pagans. God had chastened His people because of their sins. Their homeland and their temple lay in ruins. They were the shameless victims of the pagan Babylonians. Had not the Babylonians begun to believe that their gods, Marduk and Nebo, were superior to Yahweh? If the people were genuine in their repentance, would not God forgive and restore them to their land and thus vindicate His name among the heathen? Often disobedient Christians fail to recognize that their sins not only place them in jeopardy because of God's promise to chasten His erring people, but sin also brings reproach upon the name of God and gives unbelievers an excuse to question God's power and integrity.

Outline: The Prayers of Daniel

Introduction

The image of Daniel presented in the scant biographical material contained in his book reveals an exemplary and dedicated young man who learned the power and effectiveness of prayer early in his life.

A Prayer for Understanding: Daniel 2:14-23

1. The wisdom of Daniel (vv. 14-18)
2. The answer from God (v. 19a)
3. The gratitude of Daniel (vv. 19b-23)

A Prayer Confessing the People's Sin: Daniel 9:1-19

1. Daniel—a man of spiritual insight (vv. 1-3)
2. How a true believer intercedes (vv. 4-6)
3. The painful admission of guilt (vv. 7-11a)
4. Recognizing the justice of God (vv. 11b-14)
5. A plea for forgiveness and restoration (vv. 15-19)

7 PRAYERS OF JONAH

Introduction

Jonah is one of the most colorful prophets in the Old Testament. Introduced in the book that bears his name as "the son of Amittai" (1:1), Jonah was born in Gath-hepher and was a member of the tribe of Zebulun (2 Kings 14:25). Except that he seemed to have ministered during the reign of Jeroboam II in the Northern Kingdom of Israel (782-753 B.C.), all else that we know about this unusual prophet is found in the Book of Jonah.

Jonah was commissioned by God to go and preach to the people of Nineveh, a famous ancient city on the eastern bank of the Tigris River. The Bible names Asshur as the founder of Nineveh (Gen. 10:11). After the twelfth century B.C., Nineveh became one of the royal residences of Assyria. Sargon II (722-702 B.C.) named it as the capital of the Assyrian Empire, and Sennacherib (704-681 B.C.) made it a city of beauty and splendor. Great temples, palaces, and fortifications made it the chief city of the empire (2 Kings 19:36). Archaeological digs in the area have yielded not only the elaborate palace of Sennacherib but also the royal residence and famous library of Ashurbanipal in which 22,000 clay tablets were deposited. These tablets have provided scholars valuable background material for Old Testament studies.

Nineveh is such an extensive site that it may never be completely excavated.

Because of the miraculous elements contained in the Book of Jonah, it has been classified by many critics as legend, myth, or parable. Conservative theologians, however, generally see it as a valid historical account, noting that the miracles appearing in the Jonah story are among many other miracles of God that are found throughout the Old Testament, particularly in the Pentateuch. In fact, the miracles that accompanied the experience of Jonah are no more remarkable than the parting of the Red Sea and the array of miraculous events that happened during the journey of the Hebrew people from Egypt to Canaan.

Jonah shared the typical Hebrew prejudice against the Gentiles. When God instructed him to go and prophesy to the heathen Ninevites, he rebelled. Not only was such an assignment most distasteful to him personally, it would do irreparable damage to Jonah's reputation as a prophet to God's people in Israel. Jonah mistakenly felt that, if he could put distance between himself and God, he could escape the responsibility of this assignment. So he boarded a ship at Joppa, the Palestinian seaport, and began his journey toward Tarshish, believed to have been in Spain.

A violent storm arose in the course of the voyage. The captain of the ship asked Jonah to pray to his God to save them from death. But the storm continued in its fury, and the sailors aboard ship cast lots to determine if someone on board had caused the storm which they believed to be the result of divine anger. Jonah was identified as the culprit; and, at his suggestion, they reluctantly threw him into the sea. He was swallowed by a great fish prepared by God. The first of the two prayers of Jonah that we study in this chapter was prayed during the three days he spent inside the fish. Upon Jonah's repentance, God instructed the fish to cast Jonah upon the dry land, after which he went to Nineveh to carry out the mission to which God had called him earlier.

Jonah's preaching in Nineveh was effective, and, beginning with the king, the entire city repented of its gross sins. God responded by withholding the destruction of Nineveh that Jonah had predicted. Provoked that God had spared that great heathen city of the Assyrians, who were among Israel's bitterest enemies, Jonah prayed for God to take his life, which is the second of the two prayers considered in this study. The Book of Jonah is more than just the story of a disobedient prophet. It underscores the true, compassionate nature of God in His love for all people, while acknowledging the inherent prejudice of most people.

A Prayer Out of Hell

Jonah 2:1-9

The *King James Version* begins chapter 2 with "then." Perhaps there are significant implications here. Up to this point Jonah had been so determined to disobey God's call and do things his way that he probably had not prayed at all. True prayer must always contain a deference to God's will, and whatever Jonah may have said to God prior to this prayer was likely more of a complaint than an effort to secure confirmation and guidance in the matter.

Jonah's first lesson (v. 1).—Only when Jonah had reached the point of total helplessness and distress was he willing to pray. His prayer chamber was no doubt the strangest one of all time: "out of the fish's belly" (v. 1). Jonah learned that there was no place he could go to escape God's presence. David reached a similar conclusion that he expressed in one of his psalms:

> Whither shall I go from thy Spirit? or whither shall I flee from thy presence?
> If I ascend up into heaven, thou art there: if I make my bed in hell, behold, thou art there.
> If I take the wings of the morning, and dwell in the uttermost parts of the sea;
> Even there shall thy hand lead me, and thy right hand shall hold me (139: 7-10).

Jonah learned through this experience that God's presence was not limited to the boundaries of Israel. He was not a "tribal God" but, rather, the sovereign Lord of creation. There was no place Jonah could go in order to escape the all-seeing and all-knowing God.

The first step toward deliverance (vv. 2-4).—Jonah's prayer is in the form of a psalm. Including poetical passages within prose contexts is a part of normal Old Testament narrative style. To say that Jonah's experience in the fish was frightening would certainly be an understatement. For what he already had experienced aboard ship in the violent storm, ultimately being thrown overboard by the sailors upon his own insistence, was terrifying indeed. Now, whether or not Jonah realized where he was or even that he was inside a fish, he obviously had reached the conclusion as the hours passed that he was not going to die. However uncomfortable he was physically, at least he was temporarily saved from certain death. He was not going to drown in the churning sea.

Jonah realized that he had reached his extremity when he referred to his location as "the belly of hell" (v. 2). The word translated "hell" is *Sheol* in Hebrew, which was understood by the ancients to mean the grave. They believed in a hereafter, but their concept of what life was like after death was at best vague and shadowy. As far as Jonah was concerned, his back was against the wall. The only direction left for him to look was toward God. Even in the midst of the worst circumstances of his life, all of which he had brought on himself, God heard him. Twice in the opening words of his prayer psalm, Jonah referred to the fact that God "heard" him from that remote point. This awareness within Jonah brought him to the point of confession. "Yet I will look again toward thy holy temple" (v. 4). In spite of his obvious banishment from life and opportunity, in the midst of his own self-imprisonment because of his sin, Jonah determined to pray.

The terror of separation from God (vv. 5-6).—Still amazed at God's way of dealing with him, Jonah gave another description of his downward plunge into the deep and away from God. Jonah saw vividly the hopelessness of his situation. There was no way that human help could reach him. There was no "Plan B" just in case his cry to God for deliverance was not heard. Though Jonah was aware of his temporary escape from death, he apparently was resigned to the fact life as he had known it was over for him. For he said, "The earth with her bars was about me for ever" (v. 6). "Bars" refers to the Hebrew concept of "the gates of death" alluded to in Job 17:16 (NIV).

The moment of turning (vv. 7-9).—When all conscious hope for extracting himself from his dilemma was gone, Jonah "remembered the Lord." Because of his strong and deeply imbedded feelings of prejudice against the Ninevites, Jonah had to reach this extremity before he could turn toward God in confession and repentance. His statement in verse 8, "They that observe lying vanities forsake their own mercy," likely referred to the pagan sailors aboard the ship on which Jonah had been a passenger. He had a mental picture of those pagan seamen hopelessly calling on their gods. Yet Jonah, whom they doubtless thought was long since drowned in the waters of the sea, was about to experience a demonstration of God's salvation.

A Prayer of a Pouting Prophet

Jonah 4:2-3

The Jonah described in the last chapter of the book is difficult to reconcile with the repenting Jonah in chapter 2. Yet the fickleness of human nature is nowhere more clearly demonstrated than in this prayer of Jonah following the repentance of the Ninevites.

The setting of the prayer (3:3-10).—Jonah's initial responses to God's delivering him from the innards of the great fish were thanksgiving and obedience. He apparently lost no time in his journey to Nineveh. Furthermore, he began with haste his preaching campaign once he reached that great pagan metropolis. The essence of his sermon was extremely simple and to the point: "Yet forty days, and Nineveh shall be overthrown" (3:4). The powerful authority with which Jonah delivered God's message to the people was immediately effective, and the people began to repent. When the king received word of what was happening, he not only repented himself but proclaimed a citywide fast, during which the people were to pray for God's mercy in sparing them from destruction. No more beautiful picture of repentance appears in the Bible than this one of an entire city confessing its sin before God. They made no mention of the multiple gods of their pagan, polytheistic religion. They recognized the one, true God and bared their souls before Him. God's response was gracious, and His judgment of destruction predicted through the preaching of Jonah was lifted.

The unbelievable reaction of Jonah (4:1).—The reaction of God to the repentance of the heathen Ninevites was absolutely disgusting to Jonah. The Hebrew verb translated "displeased" in this verse comes from a strong expression indicating that Jonah was infuriated because of what God had done for the Ninevites. His strong reaction to God's merciful salvation extended to the Ninevites indicates that Jonah had hoped from the beginning that God would somehow destroy the city. Not only were these people Gentiles, but they were Israel's avowed enemy. Thus it was absolutely loathsome to Jonah that God had allowed the forty days to pass without obliterating those detestable Assyrians from the face of the earth! But, instead, God had heard the prayers of these people, these international outlaws, and now they had gone back to their business. Jonah forgot the many times that God had spared the Israelites when they had fallen into gross sin, and then had repented and asked for mercy. How *could* God do a thing like this?

A prayer of presumption (4:2).—Jonah admitted that, in spite of his anger at God's action, he was not really surprised at this turn of events. In fact, when God's call first came to him, while he was "yet in [his] country" (v. 2), he admitted in his own mind that God was indeed a merciful and compassionate God, who would respond to any prayer of genuine repentance and extend salvation. So, not wanting to face the possibility that the people might repent and thus trigger God's gracious response, Jonah attempted to reject God's assignment by running away.

Jonah did not want God to do what was in keeping with His merciful nature. He was not willing for God to show the Ninevites the same undeserving mercy He had shown the Israelites. His disposition was that God should punish them without giving them any opportunity to repent. Jonah reflected the feeling of his countrymen, which accounts for his desire to remain at home and minister among his own people who considered themselves "God's elite."

Jonah's way out (v. 3).—After venting his prejudicial hatred for the Assyrians in this angry prayer to God, Jonah concluded with a sigh of resignation and defeat. He prayed to die. At this point, Jonah considered death a far better option than to have to live with the knowledge that Israel's God had spared His own people's enemy. Jonah had thought that life was over for him when he asked the sailors to throw him overboard (1:12). But God had mercifully rescued him, had forgiven him for his disobedience, and had provided another opportunity for him to fulfill his divine assignment. But in spite of that, Jonah asked God to end his life. A world in which God would dare to forgive Israel's enemies was not a world Jonah wanted to live in any longer.

The tragedy of this prayer is that there is no indication in the conclusion of the book that Jonah ever changed his mind or resolved his prejudice toward the Ninevites, even though God reacted to his pouting prayer with the tender patience that a loving parent would show a frustrated child. We can only hope that, in his later years of ministry, Jonah learned the lesson of "the gourd" (4:6-11) and thus was able to conceive the richness of God's mercy and compassion.

Application

Because of the uniqueness of the Book of Jonah, it is difficult to study two prayers without involving the whole story of this reluctant prophet. Still, however, excellent applications abound in both prayers considered.

In Jonah's prayer from the fish's belly, we learn that God can hear and answer prayer no matter where or when it is prayed. God knows where His people are, whatever the circumstances are that surround them. Though Jonah was fleeing from God, he had not been cast away from God. Disobedience, however blatant, will not cause God to abandon His people. The promise is: "whom the Lord loveth he chasteneth" (Heb. 12:6). Then, the desperation of Jonah's plight took away any other possible avenue of escape which would have been a deterrent to prayer. The abiding lesson in this prayer is that no matter how deep our trouble, we can pray to God who has promised to hear us. As we rely upon Him, He manifests His power to deliver us from our distress.

The second prayer that came at the close of Jonah's ministry to Nineveh reveals the ambivalence of human nature. Even believers can show an incredible inconsistency in their attitudes toward God. Our ugly prejudices, like those of Jonah, are often the "darling sins" we secretly cherish. When they are challenged, they can reveal themselves in inconceivably unchristian ways. Our attitudes run the gamut from extreme self-pity to outright anger at God when our prayers are not answered according to our wishes. Jonah was not only foolish but impudent in his prayer conversation with God. But God was infinitely kind and gracious toward Jonah, just as He is toward us. With loving kindness, God reacted with patience toward Jonah. God had the last word in this prayer encounter. In the absence of any word concerning Jonah's response, we can only hope that he learned his lesson and allowed God to cleanse him of the despicable sin of prejudice.

Outline: The Prayers of Jonah

Introduction

The two prayers of Jonah chosen for this study provide an excellent view of the humanity of one of God's prophets. The first prayer deals with confession and repentance of sin, and the second one revealed the depths of bitterness into which a broken relationship with God can plunge a believer.

A Prayer Out of Hell: Jonah 2:1-9

1. Jonah's first lesson (v. 1)
2. The first step toward deliverance (vv. 2-4)
3. The terror of separation from God (vv. 5-6)
4. The moment of turning (vv. 7-9)

A Prayer from a Pouting Prophet: Jonah 4:2-3

1. The setting of the prayer (3:3-10)
2. The unbelievable reaction of Jonah (4:1)
3. A prayer of presumption (4:2)
4. Jonah's way out (4:3)

8 PRAYERS OF DAVID

Introduction

The names of outstanding persons call forth different responses when they are spoken. To the Hebrew, the name *Abraham* inspired a hallowed sense of privileged destiny as they saw that great man as the father of God's chosen people. *Moses* called forth feelings that approached adoration as they thought of that venerable leader who persevered forty years attempting to lead an unwieldy and often mutinous multitude of people into a land God had promised them.

But what about *David*? Ah! Few names brought forth a more universal response of love and praise than the name that graced Israel's most beloved and highly revered king—David. In the Hebrew language, the name *David* means "beloved," or possibly "chieftain." David was born in Bethlehem, the youngest son of a herdsman of that town near Jerusalem. David's father, Jesse, was a member of the tribe of Judah (1 Sam. 16:1; 2 Sam. 5:4). Jesse had seven sons older than David (1 Sam. 16:10).

David's youth was spent tending his father Jesse's flocks. He was a gifted musician, and he demonstrated his creativity by composing many of the psalms included in the Psalter. David was skilled in playing the lyre (1 Sam. 16:18), a small stringed instrument resembling a miniature harp that was used to accompany singers or poets. David was such a good musician that he was summoned to play before King Saul, the victim of frequent attacks of depression and melancholia. David played so well that Saul would forget his problems and would be relieved of his depression for the moment. Saul's condition seemed to have improved to the point that David was dismissed from the royal court and returned to his shepherding responsibilities at Bethlehem.

The stories that weave in and out of David's life are truly miracle-studded. He was noted for his courage and physical strength in killing a lion and a bear that were trying to attack his father's sheep. Then, outraged because of the cowardice of the men in Saul's army when they were challenged by the Philistine giant, Goliath, David's victorious encounter with this vain and blasphemous Philistine brought him national recognition. David was adopted into the court of King Saul and, for a time, shared in the opulence and wealth of the king's palace.

His military expertise and his growing popularity with the people resulted in King Saul's deepening jealousy and resentment toward David. Soon David was forced to become a fugitive as Saul sought to destroy him. God protected David, and following seven-and-a-half years of political strife after the death of Saul, he was anointed king of Israel (2 Sam. 2:8—5:5).

In addition to David's military and administrative skills, he organized the temple music and its singers. Perhaps his greatest contribution was composing many of the psalms. A number of them were written to express thanksgiving for God's protection during times of great danger and trauma. Other psalms, typical of the concept of retaliation and an "eye for eye, tooth for tooth " (Lev. 24:20), expressed David's desire for God to destroy his enemies. Still others were written as prayers of David's gratitude for God's glory as well as confession for his own sins. The three prayers we will examine in this chapter will show David in worship, in confession, and in thanksgiving.

A Prayer for God's Glory

Psalm 24

Old Testament people often demonstrated a rare naturalness when they communed with God in prayer. They moved between first, second, and third persons with apparent ease. They appeared at times to abandon any formality in prayer as they simply expressed their innermost thoughts to God, revealing feelings ranging from awe and worship to anger and hostility. Some of their prayers seem to fall more naturally into the category of meditation. Someone has said that "meditation is on the threshold of prayer. Hebrew meditation has crossed the border." Such is true with Psalm 24, a prayer David prayed for God's glory.

Whose world is this? (vv. 1-2.—It is a part of the human ego to enjoy the glory and praise of others because of outstanding accomplishments or achievements. Yet all of the human inventions are but discoveries of what God has already implanted in nature. We do not create anything. We merely find out God's secrets. David began this delightful prayer-psalm with an exclamation of praise in which he recognized the fundamental truth that everything began with God. The earth is that which God created, and the world represents the cultivation and production of the earth. David may have stood on a high hill and scanned the horizon before him. If he should have been at his palace window in Jerusalem's city of David, he might have seen the Mount of Olives and the distant peaks of the Judean hills. To the

east and south he could have caught sight of the Jordan Riv
er, meandering through the lush, tropical valley of Jericho,
only to empty into the brackish waters of the Dead Sea.

Not only did the physical earth and its contents belong to
God, but "the fulness thereof" and "they that dwell there
in." David understood the total ownership and sovereignty
of God and rejoiced in the glory of it!

The only way to worship (vv. 3-6).—This is that part of Da
vid's prayer-psalm that lends itself to antiphonal singing.
One choir, representing a priest perhaps, asked who was fit
to approach God in prayer. A second choir spoke for a sec
ond priest who replied that the only true candidate for an
audience with God is one whose hands are clean, whose
heart is pure, and whose soul is not vain. Hands that are
stained by such sins as murder, theft, and greed are not
qualified. Evil thoughts render the heart impure and thus
unqualified to be in God's presence.

Who is the King of Glory? (vv. 7-10).—The kingship of God
is a theme central to the Old Testament. This divine king
ship is not just a religious concept. It is a basis for worship
and praise. One cannot truly worship God without recogniz
ing His kingship and thus His absolute sovereignty.

Yet David, oriented to a military life-style, added another
dimension to this portrait of God as King. He saw King Yah
weh "strong and mighty, the Lord mighty in battle" (v. 8).
Again the Old Testament supports this concept of God also.
The "hosts" of God are often mentioned, and the suggestion
is that armies of angels are prepared to fight against and
overcome the enemies of God. Israel was a nation that had
been ravaged by war and bore the scars of those years of
anguish. The people understood the language and the pain
of war. David concluded his prayer with a victorious antici
pation of the ultimate triumph and advent of the King of
glory.

A Prayer Acknowledging Personal Sin

Psalm 32

The apostle Paul, in his synagogue sermon at Antioch of Pisidia, said of David, "He raised up unto them David to be their king; to whom also he gave testimony, and said, I have found David the son of Jesse, a man after mine own heart, which shall fulfill all my will" (Acts 13:22). No person in the Old Testament was more deeply or universally loved by his people than King David. Yet David was far from being without sin. But in spite of his imperfections, there were two major qualities that stood out concerning him. First, David willingly admitted his sin and cast himself upon the mercy of God, and second, his faith in God was consistent and strong. David genuinely desired to do God's will (see Ps. 57:7), and because of that, God made a covenant with him in which the kingdom of David was established forever. God said, "I have made a covenant with my chosen. I have sworn unto David my servant, Thy seed will I establish forever, and build up thy throne to all generations" (Ps. 89:3-4).

Psalm 32 contains a prayer of David that is drenched with tears of repentance. Along with Psalm 51, this psalm reflects upon David's dark sin of adultery and murder, involving Bathsheba and her husband, Uriah. One has only to read these two psalms to feel the wrenching pain of soul that David must have experienced because of his sin. So powerful is the message in Psalm 32 that Paul quoted the first two verses in the Epistle to the Romans (4:8). The theme of this prayer-psalm describes one of the reasons why David was indeed "a man after [God's] own heart."

The fact of sin (vv. 1-2).—David began his psalm with a general statement of thanksgiving for the person who has experienced forgiveness. He clearly believed that human beings are sinners by nature, and the only possibility of their experiencing true happiness and joy is to have their sins removed and to realize God's forgiveness.

David underscored the fact of sin by using three words to describe it. "Transgression" describes that act which consists of open rebellion against God. "Sin" is a general term that means to "miss the mark." "Iniquity" is the strongest of the three words, and it indicates distortion, criminality, and a bold disrespect for God's will. David could have used any one of these terms to describe a person's spiritual state outside of God's grace. But in order to underscore the totality of one's sin and separation from God, he used all three.

The word *guile* appears in the latter part of verse 2 and means "deceit." While this, too, is a sin, it is not grouped with the three words used previously. It is used to describe the only acceptable attitude with which one can repent of sin and expect to receive God's forgiveness—without guile (deceit). A superficial and insincere "going through the motions" of repentance will not trigger God's grace.

The pain of confession (vv. 3-4).—David described his unrepentant state as one of "silence," or the absence of confession. With symbolic and poetic terms, he portrayed the grief which characterized his miserable state. The statement "My bones waxed old through my roaring all the day long" (v. 3) shows how a person who refuses to repent of sins, after being made aware of them, suffers the pain of an accusing conscience and a weakness of spirit like that which comes physically with the aging process.

The more David determined to remain silent before God regarding his sin, to ignore it, to pretend that it did not exist, the louder his conscience screamed for relief, "roaring" inside of him. This misery was with him continually "all the day long." No answer came as a result of David's crying because his heart was still unbroken. True confession had not yet come. The agony he felt seemed to him like the heavy hand of God pressing down in punishment (38:3; 39:10). To further complicate things, the fear and depression that burned within David so tortured him that his spiritual con dition seemed like a terrible summer drought.

The result of repentance (vv. 5-7).—At last David reached the point of extremity: "the end of his rope." His heart, bat tered with the increasing awareness of what his uncon fessed sin had brought about between him and his God, was broken at last.

"I acknowledged my sin unto thee, and mine iniquity have I not hid" (v. 5). This time there was no reluctance, no holding back in David's openness before God. He "acknowl edged" or admitted what God already knew about him and had revealed to him through the painful experiences of con viction of sin. There were no secret pockets of sin in David's life that he tried to hide from God or to camouflage with excuses. With a clean sweep, he bared his soul before his Lord.

Simultaneously with David's decision to confess his sin in its totality came God's forgiveness. True repentance and God's forgiveness are so interrelated that when one repents, God instantly reciprocates with forgiveness. There is no in dication that God allowed David to suffer a moment longer in his miserable state. Prior to this point, David's words to God had been those of a petulant child who had been caught in his sins and was trying desperately to justify or excuse himself. Now the tone changes. Prior to his repentance, Da vid's praying had sounded like the discordant notes of an orchestra whose instruments were not only out of tune but whose players were not following the score. Now, because of the genuineness of his repentance, the clear tones of joy poured from David's soul with beautiful harmony and melody. They became a musical "yea and amen" to the truth of God's available grace.

David quickly shared the truth that what had happened to him was available to everyone who would call upon God as he had done (v. 6). He had found a "golden nugget" in the forgiving response of God. He did not hide what he had found. Now others, suffering as he had suffered under the guilt of sin, could make the same discovery. Furthermore, God had become a "hiding place" (v. 7), or a place of refuge, for David. A little while before an unrepentant David had chafed because of God's chastening. Now he found a shelter in God, whose full forgiveness had replaced His wrath. David felt as if he was encircled by the ecstatic music of God's mercy and grace.

A word from the Lord (vv. 8-9).—God responded to David's prayer by assuring him that he would be taught how to live, and as long as David walked faithfully in the path God marked out for him, he would find divine protection. Note that God did not infer that David would never again experience temptation or conflict. God would not be a buffer against all exposure to ungodly influences. Rather strength would be provided in the knowledge David received regarding how to live.

A wise conclusion (vv. 10-11).—Out of painful experience David drew upon the lessons he had learned from his sin. The sorrow that came to him because he had broken God's law and thus had interrupted his relationship with the Lord seemed to have spawned "many sorrows." But when he confessed his sin and repented, God's mercy surrounded him. Once again he was righteous before God and was able to rejoice and "shout for joy" (v. 11). Such an experience is available to anyone who will do as David did.

A Prayer Answered

Psalm 40

David wrote this psalm after he had experienced some great distress or trouble. It includes a moving section in which he thanked God for answering prayer. There is no way of knowing for certain what crisis he had in mind. It could have been one of the occasions when King Saul and his men were pursuing David with the intent to kill him. Or it may have been prayed upon his deliverance from a sense of guilt resulting from his own personal sin and disobedience toward God. Whatever it was, David felt compelled to share the refreshing experience one has when a definite prayer is answered, and fellowship with God is restored.

A personal thanksgiving (vv. 1-3).—Through his prayer experiences with God, David had learned patience. Typical of the astute military strategist, David was accustomed to things happening in response to his commands. His sovereign authority as king would even enhance his power over others as well as over events. It would be natural, then, that when David prayed, he would expect God to answer his prayers as quickly as his subordinates responded to his orders. But God did not choose to function that way with David. The king needed to learn patience and submission. Humility and royalty were characteristically incompatible. Yet God would teach David lessons that would create a capacity for both patience and humility.

The experience out of which God had delivered David was so traumatic it seemed to him that he was caught irretrievably in slimy clay in the bottom of "an horrible pit" (v. 2). We can imagine all kinds of awesome conditions suggested by such a pit. But in answer to David's cry for help, God not only had rescued him from that pit, but God had "set [his] feet upon a rock, and established [his] goings" (v. 2). The "rock" suggests the antithesis of the slimy clay from the standpoint of stability and balance. Uncertainty produced by a condition David may have considered hopeless at the time caused him not only to lose his self-confidence but also his sense of direction. The "rock" upon which God had placed him not only restored his confidence in God and in himself as God's man, but also it gave him a *new* sense of direction which he could follow with assurance.

Being the natural musician that David was, he could not resist singing "a new song" whose text was praise to God for what He had done. David's song not only would allow the joyful expression of gratitude from his own soul, but it would serve as a testimony before those who did not know God, or if they acknowledged His being, they had not come to the point of trusting in Him.

God's goodness to His people (vv. 4-5)—Those who *do* place their hope and trust in God are assured of happiness. This state of joy comes not when confidence is placed in "the proud," those who would exalt and congratulate themselves for whatever victories have come to them. For one to take credit for whatever good things come is to "turn aside to lies" (v. 4). For the truth is: "Every good gift and every perfect gift is from above, and cometh down from the Father of lights, with whom is no variableness, neither shadow of turning" (Jas. 1:17). Suddenly, when David tried to think of the many ways in which God had blessed him, he was overwhelmed. The task of trying to number them all was far too great for his limited memory.

Dedication to God's will (vv. 6-10).—As David stood in awe of the goodness of God to him, he realized that the ritual of sacrifices and offerings in themselves would never satisfy God until His people determined to seek after and follow the divine will with all their hearts. The Old Testament sacrifices and offerings were designed to teach the people what kind of a relationship God wanted with them, and also to point toward a coming Redeemer who would fulfill once and for all the need for those religious acts. God would write His law in the *hearts* of His people, and they would realize and practice a new relationship with Him. Because God had revealed this glorious truth to David, he had been faithful to pass it on to his people. He had held back nothing that God had revealed to him.

A prayer for deliverance (vv. 11-17).—David concluded his psalm by looking briefly toward the future and realizing that other crises would be imminent. He was no longer burdened with unconfessed sin. He enjoyed a healthy spiritual relationship with God. At the same time, he realized that situations produced by former sinful acts, though now forgiven by God, might still have contributed to present and future problems and crises. So again David pleaded for deliverance. Yet David's plea did not include the lack of assurance and confidence he had expressed earlier before he experienced God's forgiveness and a renewed sense of His presence. For David's concluding statement (vv. 16-17) confirmed his confidence that God was with him, as He will be with all who seek Him and love His salvation.

Application

In choosing the prayers of the various individuals thus far, an attempt has been made to show the humanity of these persons as they experienced their spiritual mood swings from immaturity, even gross sin, to repentance, faith, and spiritual strength. The three prayers of David considered in this chapter again show three facets of his developing personality.

The first prayer (Ps. 24) deals with David's growing

awareness of the glory of God, acknowledging Him as Creator of the earth and as Sovereign Lord. The quality of our worship will be determined by our awareness of the greatness and glory of our God. The popular, overfamiliarity with God projected by some takes away from His glory and tends to reduce Him to a "buddy" God who would be soft on sin. David also learned something of the stewardship of God's children with the realization that God is the true owner of all things. The earth as we know it is His by creation. We, too, need to learn that we are but stewards of what God has allowed us to have, and we are accountable to Him for our possessions and how we use them. Worshiping God is a total experience, the result of which affects all that a person is and does.

Psalm 32 provides an excellent lesson in confession of sin, repentance, and divine forgiveness. The truths David revealed in this prayer acknowledging his sin sound as though he and Paul had compared notes! David's conclusion was that forgiveness is totally a matter of God's reckoning. We do not manipulate or coerce divine forgiveness. The relationship established between a repentant sinner and a forgiving God is a matter of human trust in God's unchanging love. Because of what David experienced when he confessed his sin and received God's forgiveness, his heart was filled with a new song. Joy is uniquely a Christian experience, for it is based on a state of being and not upon circumstances. When sinners relinquish their guilt to God in confession of sin, they are set free to enjoy God's love.

Psalm 40 is David's expression of gratitude for answered prayer in the past and a plea for God's help in coping with crises that are sure to come. Often we tend to forget past answers to prayer in the frustrations that overwhelm us regarding present troubles. Reflection on answered prayer fortifies us with assurance that the God who heard us yesterday never changes, but He is the same yesterday, today, and forever. Also, David found that when he thought of God's past blessings, he was impressed to share them with others. Thus an evangelistic opportunity was provided. God's people have much for which to be thankful. We should not repress our gratitude but express it to others as opportunities arise. "Let the redeemed of the Lord say so"! (Ps. 107:2).

Outline: Prayers of David

Introduction

David, referred to by the apostle Paul as "a man after [God's] own heart," was one of the most colorful and, at times, unpredictable characters in the Old Testament. He was often tempted, and sometimes he yielded to temptation. He was a sinner and a saint. But he confessed his sin and repented, and God honored his integrity with many blessings.

A Prayer for God's Glory: Psalm 24

1. Whose world is this? (vv. 1-2)
2. The only way to worship (vv. 3-6)
3. Who is the King of glory? (vv. 7-10)

A Prayer Acknowledging Personal Sin: Psalm 32

1. The fact of sin (vv. 1-2)
2. The pain of confession (vv. 3-4)
3. The result of repentance (vv. 5-7)
4. A word from the Lord (vv. 8-9)
5. A wise conclusion (vv. 10-11)

A Prayer Answered: Psalm 40

1. A personal thanksgiving (vv. 1-3)
2. God's goodness to His people (vv. 4-5)
3. Dedication to God's will (vv. 6-10)
4. A prayer for deliverance (vv. 11-17)

9 PRAYERS OF PAUL

Introduction

C. S. Lewis, one of the most brilliant Christian advocates and writers of modern times, was an agnostic in the early years of his adult life. But the unrelenting prodding of the Holy Spirit finally penetrated his wall of resistance, touched his seeking mind, and led him to face the reality of God's existence. But still Lewis struggled. His human reason wrestled with the miraculous aspects of Christianity. Then one day he surrendered and entered the kingdom of God and the family of the redeemed through faith in Jesus Christ. Of his experience Lewis later said, "I entered the Kingdom of God kicking and screaming!"

This was much the experience of Paul in his conversion. Of course, salvation experiences differ from person to person. With some, accepting Christ—leaving the old life and entering the new—is as peaceful and serene as a summer sunset. It is like the graceful opening of an exquisite bud into full flower. This is not to say that there was not the spiritual tension of rebirth. But the battle was won quickly, and the trauma was minimal.

But with others, the exit from the kingdom of darkness and entrance into the Kingdom of light resulted in a full-scale war. For the resistance of the human will varies from individual to individual. Often this struggle is most violent *not* when one leaves a life of immorality and sin but when one is a decent, law-abiding, and even devotedly "religious" person—but not a Christian!

Such was the case with the apostle Paul. If sincerity is the criterion for preparing one for heaven, Paul—the Pharisee, the rabbi, and the persecutor of Christians—would have been assured a front-row seat there! Paul possessed a genuine religious zeal. He was totally sincere in religious matters. In short, Paul's life was the sad picture of a person with misdirected zeal.

A number of events figured into the process God used to bring Paul to the point of confrontation. One of these was his encounter with Stephen, one of the seven men the early church appointed to help the apostles by taking care of the physical and material needs of the church. This released the apostles to spend more time praying and preaching. Stephen appears to have been the most vocal and visible of these men. He was determined to express his faith in Christ and implement his vision for spreading the gospel. Stephen was a Hellenistic Jew. He had been born and reared outside of Palestine. Such Jews had been "hellenized," which meant they had been exposed to the Greek culture in other parts of the world. Many of them could not even speak Hebrew, the sacred language of the Old Testament and of the Judean Jews. Most of these Hellenistic Jews observed the Commandments and, other than the language, they had not abandoned their Jewish faith. They continued to return to Jerusalem each year for the great feast weeks of Judaism.

Two things were especially precious to the Jews. First, the temple in Jerusalem was hallowed because there they believed God dwelt exclusively in the holy of holies. At the temple alone could God be worshiped and sacrifices offered to Him. Then second, the Jews revered the law of Moses, which stood as an unchangeable bulwark in their minds. But Stephen saw that the temple must pass away, and the law of Moses was but a "schoolmaster" to teach people what sin really is and how it is impossible for one, in one's own strength and goodness, to keep the law. He saw the law of the Old Testament as being a preparatory stage for Christianity, that proclaims the grace of God in providing the free gift of salvation for *all* who would believe, both Jew *and* Gentile.

Apparently, Paul had heard Stephen, the persuasive and Spirit-filled Christian Jew, speak in one of the synagogues attended by the Hellenistic Jews (for Paul himself, born in Tarsus of Cilicia, was a Hellenistic Jew). He may have heard Stephen declare that God did *not* dwell in a temple made with hands, but that He lived in the hearts of His people. But the crowning blow that sealed Stephen's destiny in Paul's mind was his insistence that the Jews' crucifixion of Jesus was only a continuation of what they had done throughout their history. They had persecuted and destroyed the prophets who had faced them with their sins and with the purpose God had for their very existence. These were stinging words for a people who believed they were God's exclusive, chosen people, above and beyond all others.

So the death warrant for Stephen was issued. The piercing conviction of God's Spirit on the wings of Stephen's words had ravaged the hearts of his fellow Jews. In order to safeguard their own religious pride and traditions, they had to destroy Stephen. And this is where Paul first appeared on the scene. When the executors prepared to stone Stephen, Luke stated that "the witnesses laid down their clothes at a young man's feet, whose name was Saul" (Acts 7:58). As Paul stood there, custodian of the coats of the stoners, he heard Stephen pray, "Lord, lay not this sin to their charge"

(Acts 7:60). Paul may have seen something on Stephen's face as he looked into heaven and "saw the glory of God, and Jesus standing on the right hand of God" (Acts 7:55). For the rest of his life, Paul was not able to erase that scene from his memory.

After that, Paul committed himself more fanatically than ever to destroying the church. The great persecution of the church broke out with the martyrdom of Stephen, and Paul was the front-runner in leading it. Yet God was glorified even in the midst of the persecution, for wherever the believers went, they shared their faith. Fellowships of Christian believers were springing up everywhere. When one "fire" would be temporarily extinguished, another would break out somewhere else. Paul's strategy was not so much to destroy the Christians, thus making them martyrs, but he committed himself to making them deny Christ and blaspheme His name publicly. He discovered, instead, that Christ's true followers had rather die than deny their Lord. Paul's zeal became like a raging fire within him, driving him out of Judea and Samaria into foreign lands in his mad pursuit of Christians. It was when he was en route to Damascus in Syria that Paul was "arrested" by God in a vision. His confrontation with the risen Lord Jesus in that heavenly vision resulted in his conversion to Christianity. The same burning zeal with which Paul had persecuted Christians and sought to destroy the church was miraculously redirected, and he became the great pioneer for spreading the gospel of Christ beyond the borders of Palestine to the Gentile world. In this chapter, we will study three recorded prayers of Paul that reveal something of the personality and commitment of this great apostle of the Lord Jesus Christ.

A Prayer of Conversion

Acts 9:1-6,11

Paul's prayer of conversion stands out as one of the amazing examples of God's sovereignty in the life of an individual. No doubt the Holy Spirit had been at work in His convicting ministry in Paul's life before this climactic moment. However, Paul still was committed to what he believed to be the will of God; to eradicate this splinter group of people within Judaism who were followers of Jesus of Nazareth. With total sincerity and honesty, Paul considered them heretics who posed a serious threat to the "true religion" of Judaism. But God had been at work in Paul's life from before his birth, according to the apostle's own testimony (Gal. 1:15-16). The experience on the Damascus Road was merely the acting out in history of that which was God's will in Paul's life.

The growth of the early church (vv. 1-2).—In his determination to stamp out Christianity, Paul had secured warrants from the high priest, with the sanction of the Sanhedrin, to travel to Damascus and arrest any followers of Christ who may have been associated with the synagogue there. This was a civil and religious right the Roman government permitted the Jews to exercise concerning members of their own race. For the first time, the disciples of Christ, who were not yet called Christians, were referred to as being "of this way" (9:2). This designation of believers appears five other times in the Book of Acts (19:9,23; 22:4; 24:14,22).

The Divine intervention (vv. 3-4).—Paul's visit to Damascus indicates how widely Christianity had spread by this time. As Paul neared Damascus, the light of God's glory suddenly flashed forth. Luke called it simply "a light from heaven" (v. 3). In one of the personal accounts of his conversion experience, Paul referred to it as "a light from heaven, brighter than the sun" (26:13, RSV). The impact was such that Paul fell to the ground. Simultaneously with the light came the sound of a voice saying, "Saul, Saul, why persecutest thou me?" (v. 4). This startling question reflected that Paul's battle was truly not against the Christians but against God in the Person of His Son.

The startled response (vv. 5-6).—In response to the question, Paul asked, "Who art thou, Lord?" Some believe that Paul used the word *lord* not in a worshipful way but as a means of courteous or polite address, as often was the custom in ancient times. It seems more reasonable, however, seeing that Paul had been struck down so dramatically by the bright light, that he would have assumed naturally that the voice also came from heaven and indicated the divine presence. At this point Paul probably was thoroughly confused. Paul could not understand why he was being rebuked by God for doing what he thought was God's work. So bewildered was Paul that, not knowing what else to say, he blurted out this question asking for God's true identity. Could it be possible that He was *not* the God Paul had always thought He was?

No doubt Paul was stunned by what he heard next: "I am Jesus whom thou persecutest" (v. 5). In one shattering moment of time, Paul was forced to identify the Lord God of the Old Testament, whom he believed he had been serving zealously, with Jesus of Nazareth whom he had been persecuting in the persons of His followers. Totally shaken and religiously disoriented, Paul stammered, "Lord, what wilt thou have me to do?" (v. 6). This, no doubt, was Paul's moment of new birth. Just as physical birth is accompanied by agonizing pain, so is spiritual birth the most radical and cataclysmic experience a person can have. Paul, the self-controlled, intensely religious Pharisee suddenly became the dependent, subservient follower of Christ!

Paul's instructions were clear and to the point. He was to enter Damascus, and when he arrived in the city, he would be told what he "must do" (v. 6). Already, Paul had to exercise faith. He was not told ahead of time what awaited him in Damascus. Paul may have remembered another man, named Abraham, whose instructions were to act without being provided with an agenda for what lay ahead. The spiritual shock was so traumatic to Paul that it resulted in a temporary physical blindness that lasted three days, during which he neither ate nor drank. During that time Paul waited in Damascus, which was another demonstration of faith required of him.

The incredible timing (v. 11).—At the same time, God was speaking to Ananias, a Jew of Damascus who was a believer in Jesus. Whether or not Ananias was a leader of Christ's followers in Damascus, apparently he was submissive enough to God's will to be the human instrument God chose to use to guide Paul in further understanding what had happened to him (v. 11). The sovereignty of God was supreme in Paul's conversion experience, yet still a human response was required. Paul's prayer of conversion unlocked the door of his heart from *his* side, opening his life to the flow of God's saving power.

A Prayer for Deliverance

2 Corinthians 12:1-10

The record of Paul's prayer for deliverance is one of the most intimate and personal interludes of his Christian life. It is *so* private that Paul did not record the actual words that he prayed, thus we have no record of the dilemma in his life that prompted the prayer. He did tell us what brought about this experience in his life.

The dilemma (vv. 1-7).—In the opening verses of chapter 12, Paul wrote about an experience in which he was caught up into "paradise," where he heard things he could not tell (v. 4). Then, lest he feel superior to his fellow believers because of that rare experience, God allowed something to happen in his life that he likened to a "messenger of Satan to buffet me" (v. 7). He also compared this experience to "a thorn in the flesh." Though Paul lived an exemplary Christian life, he was human and vulnerable to temptation. He also knew that the closer people walk with God, the more intense will be Satan's efforts to convince them of their superiority to their fellow believers. God had blessed Paul singularly with this visionary visit to heaven. The setting for self-exaltation was a natural one.

Paul used two figures of speech with which to describe God's method of protecting him from the sin of self-righteousness in this instance. First, he likened it to "a thorn in the flesh." The word translated "thorn" describes a sharply pointed sliver. A splinter or thorn like this can cause persistent pain, even infection and swelling. When one has a splinter or thorn in any part of the body, the natural impulse is to remove it at once, thus stopping the pain and the possibility of infection.

The second figure of speech Paul used was a "messenger of Satan to buffet me," which actually enforced the comparison to the thorn. The word translated "buffet" means fisticuffs. Paul did not elaborate on the nature of this troubling thing God permitted in his life. Bible students have made numerous suggestions, ranging from an eye disease or malaria to epilepsy. Others even think Paul may have been married, and upon his conversion to Christianity his wife refused to join him in his faith in Christ. None of these sug-gestions are necessarily valid. The safest approach is to hon-or Paul's apparent decisions to keep the details private.

The reaction (v. 8).—Paul did not say when this problem came into his life although, based on the reference to the experience in paradise, many believe it happened soon after that revelation. Paul noted that he prayed three times that the Lord might remove the problem from his life. *Three times* also means that Paul received his answer from the Lord three times. His praying most likely was not a persis-tent effort to coax God to act contrary to His will. At this point in Paul's spiritual journey, it would be ridiculous to think he would so misunderstand God's way of dealing with His children that he would pray *any* prayer other than one that acquiesced to God's will. Surely Paul had an excellent grasp on the principles of true petitionary prayer.

The promise (vv. 9-10).—God promised Paul that His grace was sufficient for every need in his life, whether it related to his work, his suffering, or to this particular dis-tressing thing that harassed him. *Grace* is one of the golden nuggets in the Bible as it relates to God's undeserved favor toward one who is a sinner. God's grace bestows both pardon and peace and provides support and deliverance. It brings comfort, strength, assurance, hope, and joy unspeakable.

Paul's conclusion, after having received this assurance from God, was that his attitude toward this troubling prob-lem reversed. He rejoiced because he realized the end result would be the power of Christ released through him. This nagging thorn would keep him constantly aware of the weakness of the flesh and of his vulnerability to sin. By de-nying himself, Paul would become a channel through which God's blessings could flow to others.

A Prayer for Inner Growth

Ephesians 3:14-21

Paul was an evangelist *par excellence*, and his burning desire was to introduce everyone to Christ with the passion that they come to know Him as Savior. Yet his desire did not stop there. He longed to grow in spiritual strength himself and to see those whom he had led to Christ experience inner growth also. In Paul's letter to the Ephesians, he referred to an earnest prayer he prayed in this regard.

A humble supplication (vv. 14-15).—With deepest reverence, Paul offered this prayer for inner growth. He knew and taught that the miracle changing a person's spiritual status from darkness to light was instantaneous. But the process by which one grows as a believer is a continuing one. Many obstacles will be encountered by the individuals who commit themselves to this inner spiritual development.

An amazing progression (vv. 16-19).—Paul noted five ways in which this progressive, moral change in a believer's life is brought about. First, it happens by the strengthening of one's inward spiritual life; second, by the dwelling of Christ in one's heart; third, by this firm foundation in love; fourth, by experiencing the love of Christ, and fifth, by being "filled with all the fullness of God" (v. 19).

All of this happens as Christ takes up residence in a person's heart, and is allowed to be "Lord" of the decisions and actions of that individual. This becomes a continuously developing state as the believer keeps on trusting Christ. Paul did not have a "static" position in mind here but rather a maintained, fresh experience. When Paul prayed that Christ may "dwell in your hearts by faith" (v. 17), he was thinking of the mind, the emotions, the will, or of the totality of one's being.

A majestic benediction (vv. 20-21).—This doxology may be the most beautiful and sublime of any appearing in Paul's letters. It appears as the climax of the first half of the Ephesian letter, and it is perhaps the spiritual peak of the entire epistle. For after chapter 3, Paul appeared to concentrate on practical matters of Christian living. Actually, in this doxology Paul rehearsed themes he had already touched upon earlier in the letter. He dealt with the abundance of God's gift, which is the fullness of His presence made available to His people. This gift is made possible through His limitless power continually working within the lives of believers. Furthermore, the scope of what is available to believers from God's store of blessings is far beyond what could ever be imagined or expressed.

In verse 21 Paul spoke of God's love for His church in that He has vested His glory there in the Person of His Son, Jesus Christ. The church's glorious privilege is to honor the Lord Jesus Christ through the individual lives and testimonies of its members. To no other earthly institution or entity has God delegated that privilege and responsibility. This function of the body of Christ, the church, will last forever, "world without end." Throughout eternity, the church, the bride of Christ, will exalt her Savior and Bridegroom, the Lord Jesus Christ.

Application

These three prayers of Paul represent three different facets of this remarkable man's spiritual journey. The first one appears at the beginning of his Christian experience and describes in vivid detail his moment of conversion. Before this actual moment when Paul's soul was transferred from the kingdom of darkness to the Kingdom of light, the Holy Spirit had been laying the groundwork for the miracle of conversion in Paul's life. God works this way in the life of everyone who receives Christ as Savior. True enough, the miracle of regeneration is instantaneous, but the preparation and cultivation for that moment is progressive. The length of time varies with the individual. Sometimes, as was true with Paul, the time factor is lengthy, depending on the willingness of the individual to respond.

Another important truth to be realized in Paul's conversion is the uniqueness of each person's experience. Some are radical and dramatic whereas others appear more quiet and serene. Yet the miracle of spiritual change is the same. No one should question or evaluate one's personal conversion on the basis of another person's experience.

The second prayer, dealing with Paul's "thorn in the flesh," reveals the humanity of the great apostle and describes the ongoing struggle he faced with temptation and satanic harassment in his life. Few Christians, if any, escape such experiences in their lives. Based on Paul's record of his dilemma, we can conclude that God permits these troubling interludes in our lives in order to cause us to exercise our faith and strengthen our dependence on Him. Most of the time, the ultimate prayer in such instances is for God's will to be done, whatever the particular outcome may be. As with Paul, His word to us will be that His strength is made "perfect" or complete in the midst of our weakness.

The third prayer, Paul's prayer for inner growth in his life as well as in the lives of fellow believers, represents the apostle's continuing concern for spiritual development. Growing in God's grace and in the knowledge of the Lord Jesus Christ was a priority in Paul's thinking and teaching. Attention to "the inner man" (v. 16) was the focus of Paul's concern for those whom he had introduced to Christ in the churches throughout Asia Minor and eastern Europe.

Paul longed to experience a continually deepening understanding of the love and power of God. Furthermore, Paul recognized that it was the responsibility and privilege of the church to honor the Lord Jesus Christ in all of its activities and ministries. This should be a continuing priority in every fellowship of believers. Every program and ministry of the church should either directly or indirectly bring glory to Christ, or else the ultimate goal of the church will not be realized.

Outline: Prayers of Paul

Introduction

Though we tend to view the life of the apostle Paul as being miracle-studded from beginning to end, we must not lose sight of the humanity of this great pioneer of the faith. These three prayers point out Paul's struggle to grow as a Christian as he worked through personal dilemmas and distresses comparable to those that affect every believer.

A Prayer of Conversion: Acts 9:1-6,11

1. The growth of the early church (vv. 1-2)
2. The divine intervention (vv. 3-4)
3. The startled response (vv. 5-6). God's incredible timing (v. 11)

A Prayer for Deliverance: 2 Corinthians 12:7-10

1. The dilemma (vv. 1-7)
2. The reaction (v. 8)
3. The promise (vv. 9-10)

A Prayer for Inner Growth: Ephesians 3:14-21

1. A humble supplication (vv. 14-15)
2. An amazing progression (vv. 16-19)
3. A majestic benediction (vv. 20-21)

10 PRAYERS OF JESUS

Introduction

There is no way one can compare the prayers of Jesus with the prayers of believers. When *we* pray, we are limited by the natural weaknesses of our humanity. We cannot see into the future, nor can we always understand the present. Nor do we always pray with wisdom and discernment. Often we ask for those things which are not within the will of God, and thus would not be good for us. Our prayers occasionally are selfish—designed to manipulate God's intervention for the purpose of serving our own interests.

Jesus' prayers recorded in the Gospels were examples of His communication with His Heavenly Father. While there was a self-limited dimension to Jesus' earthly life, He still reflected the perfection and omniscience of God. He was the God-Man, perfect God and perfect Man. The only prayer of Jesus recorded in Holy Scripture that relates to His humanity is the prayer He prayed in the Garden of Gethsemane, the third of the three prayers of Jesus we will examine in this study.

Jesus' disciples were amazed and fascinated by Jesus' praying. As Jews, they were accustomed to the formal, written prayers of Judaism. Many of the Psalms are prayers prayed by their authors, representing various stages in their spiritual experiences and growth. Spontaneous prayer actually was foreign to the Jews. To address God intimately as Jesus did, or as a child would address his or her father, was foreign to them. Probably such a personal approach to prayer would have been considered presumptuous, if not downright blasphemous.

Jesus often went alone into the mountains to pray where He would continue in prayer with His Heavenly Father all night. The disciples were aware of this, and they were puzzled that Jesus would feel it necessary to spend such extended periods of time in prayer. One day one of His disciples, speaking for the rest of them, asked Him to teach them to pray "as John also taught his disciples" (Luke 11:1). John's disciples, thoroughgoing Jews, were accustomed to prayer in the context of Judaism. But John the Baptist taught his disciples to pray in a special way that went beyond what Judaism had taught them. Jesus, in turn, went beyond John's revelation and taught *His* disciples by His words and His example.

The three prayers in this chapter, chosen from the Gospels' accounts of Jesus' public ministry, take three different approaches to prayer as Jesus taught and practiced it. First, there is the Model Prayer He included in the Sermon on the Mount, then His priestly prayer (which is truly "the *Lord's* prayer"), and finally, the highly personal prayer of agony He prayed in the garden of Gethsemane.

A Model Prayer

Matthew 6:9-13

Realizing that much wrong information and demonstration existed about prayer, Jesus took great pains to teach His disciples its true meaning and essence. He prefaced the profoundly simple Model Prayer with His condemnation of the hypocritical praying of those who stood in the synagogues and on the streets to pray, thus parading their piety before those who observed them. He mentioned also the meaningless babbling of the heathens who, like the prophets of Baal in Elijah's day, thought their gods would hear them because of "their much speaking" (v. 7).

The "how" of prayer (v. 9*a*).—When Jesus said, "After this manner therefore pray ye," He used the present imperative tense of the verb. A literal translation would be, "In this manner, therefore, be praying." His point was that the spirit reflected in the Model Prayer was to characterize *all* of their praying. Clearly, however, Jesus intended for this prayer to be only a model. He was saying, as it were, "This is *how,* not *what,* you are to pray." This prayer was totally opposite from the ostentatious praying of the hypocrites or the thoughtless, meaningless praying of the heathen.

The Model Prayer Jesus gave His disciples was perfect in every respect. No human prayer could ever equal it. Also, the words *this* and *you* in this verse are both emphatic, suggesting that this is a prayer that can be prayed in faith only to the God who sent Jesus as the Messiah and Savior of the world. Thus, one who does not recognize Jesus as Messiah cannot use this prayer as a true model for praying.

Our relationship to God and to His Kingdom (vv. 9*b*-10).— Only a true child of God can address Him as "Father," and it is only by faith in Christ that one can be made a child of God. "Our Father" draws the Almighty God down to us, but locating Him "in heaven" acknowledges His eternal greatness. Jesus did not mean to suggest that God dwells *only* in the heavens (the plural form of heaven is used here). Because God is omnipresent, His presence is everywhere.

Also, there is the concept of *community* in the plural pronoun *our.* We pray by faith to a God whom we cannot see, and, in community, we experience the love of God that binds us together. As we anticipate heaven, there is the element of hope. Thus faith, hope, and love are inseparably joined in the first petition of the Model Prayer.

"Hallowed," the verb form of *holy*, means that which is set apart from everything common or profane. God's "name" is not a mere sound or concept revealed to us. It is a reflection of who God is. To pray that God's name be "hallowed" is not to pray for His name to become holy but that it be treated as holy. Those who have been created in God's image should never despise His name, but recognize it for the holiness it represents.

The "kingdom" is the heavenly reign and rule of God through Christ. It is always "coming" in the sense of its realization in the lives of those who receive Christ as Savior. But the anticipation of believers is its consummation in the return of Christ to reign on earth. Thus God's kingdom embraces two spheres. Today we know it as God's rule of grace. Upon one's salvation, God begins His rule within the individual's heart. When Christ returns, however, we shall know the kingdom as God's rule of glory. For then, faith will be realized. "For now we see through a glass, darkly; but then face to face: now I know in part; but then shall I know even as also I am known" (1 Cor. 13:12).

To pray that God's "will be done in earth, as it is in heaven" (v. 10) is a broad and all-embracing petition. God's "will" includes the righteous demands of God along with His determination to bring about certain events in salvation history. So this request is that God's will be done *now,* on earth, as it is being done in heaven, and that it be as fully accomplished on earth as it is in heaven. The consummation of God's will, of course, is the bringing in of the messianic kingdom on earth. This petition, then, embraces that ultimate goal.

Our relationship to ourselves, to our needs, and to others (vv. 11-13).—Though one's eternal soul is the most important part of the being, the Scriptures never minimize the significance of the physical body. The apostle Paul reminded us that the body is the "temple of the Holy Spirit" (1 Cor. 6:19, RSV). "Our daily bread" represents our least but often most troublesome needs. We are to be satisfied with God's provision for today and not be overly concerned about tomorrow. Generally, God gives us abundantly more than we need for each day.

"Forgive us our debts" means, literally, to dismiss from us our sins. Luke, in his account of the Model Prayer, refers to "debts" as "sins" (Luke 11:4). God has promised, upon our repentance, to send our sins as far from Him as "the east is from the west" (Ps. 103:12). Furthermore, our realization of God's grace in forgiving *our* sins should have a positive bearing on the attitudes we have toward those who sin against us. The way in which we forgive others is evidence that God's forgiving grace has been experienced in our lives.

After acknowledging our past sins and our need for forgiveness, we next are to turn to possible future sins that would tempt us. Often temptation comes in the trappings of harmless, innocent situations. What would tempt one person to sin may be no temptation at all to another. So this petition is asking the Heavenly Father to take charge of our lives and shield us from those situations which our faith is not strong enough to overcome. Not only does the believer deplore the possibility of falling victim to temptation, one also shrinks away from that which would bring dishonor to the Lord.

The last petition in the prayer, "Deliver us from evil" (v. 13), looks forward to a final release from this world whose atmosphere is saturated with evil. All moral wickedness is referred to here, and the anticipation is that the time will come when all opposition from Satan, the god of this world, will be swept away forever. It is the final petition because, when it is granted, we shall need nothing more.

The prayer concludes with a threefold benediction or doxology. "Thine is the kingdom, and the power, and the glory, for ever" (v. 13). His is the kingdom, and we are the subjects. His power represents His authority over all things, and His glory affirms the truth that He is the only One worthy of our eternal worship and adoration.

A Priestly Prayer

John 17

It may have been somewhere near the midnight hour on Thursday before His crucifixion the next day when Jesus prayed this prayer. There is a spot today, at the foot of the Mount of Olives, where one can stand facing the east and see the summit of that historic old mountain. Then, looking toward the west, there is in plain view the Eastern Gate in the wall surrounding the ancient city of Jerusalem. Beyond the gate there is the gold dome of the Moslem shrine built on the traditional spot where the hallowed Jewish Temple once stood. We do not know where Jesus was when He prayed this remarkable prayer. He and His disciples may have been somewhere between the upper room in Jerusalem where they had observed the Passover meal together, and the garden of Gethsemane at the foot of the Mount of Olives.

Jesus may have been at or near this spot where He could see the gleaming white marble of the Temple, lighted by the torches flaming on the Temple courts, and at the same time He could see the ominous, black outline of the Mount of Olives looming toward the east. If it was indeed the midnight hour, the people of Jerusalem were sleeping, oblivious to the momentous events and struggles that were taking place both in heaven and on earth at that very moment.

Jesus and His disciples were physically and emotionally drained. The disciples were practically in a state of shock because of all that Jesus had said to them that night. He had compressed into five or six hours some of the hardest and most challenging words He had ever spoken to them. Then, all of a sudden, Jesus started to pray. The disciples had heard Him pray before, but never had they seen Him like this, or heard Him pray in this manner. This prayer is truly "the Lord's Prayer" and should be carefully distinguished from the Model Prayer recorded in Matthew 6 and Luke 11. Martin Luther said that Jesus prayed this prayer so that He might carry out His office as our *only* High Priest.

Christ prayed for Himself (vv. 1-5).—Jesus was always conscious of living by God's calendar. Often, during His earthly ministry, He said, "Mine hour is not yet come." Jesus knew that, at last, the hour had come for Him to fulfill to the last "jot" and "tittle" (Matt. 5:18), the reason for His coming to earth. "Glorify thy Son," He prayed to His Father. For thirty-three years Jesus had lived within the natural limitations of His human nature. He "was in all points tempted like as we are, yet without sin" (Heb. 4:15). Now, as He was approaching the climactic moment of all time and eternity, the offering of His life as the sinless Sacrifice for mankind's sins, Jesus prayed that He be filled with the fullness of God's glory.

Christ had glorified His Father in that He had revealed the Father's true attributes. He had "brought God near" to people in revealing Him not as an unapproachable Deity, who delighted in lashing out in judgment toward those who broke His Commandments, but as a God of love who longed to be reconciled with His sinful people. Christ would be glorified in His resurrection and again upon His return to earth.

Christ prayed for His disciples (vv. 6-19).—It is indeed good news that Christ prays for those who are His. A major function of His presence in heaven now at the right hand of the Father is "to make intercession" for the saints (Heb. 7:25). At this point in His prayer, however, He did not pray for the "world." He was about to *die* for sinners. His intercession was for those who are His by faith in His atoning work on the cross. Then Jesus prayed specifically for His disciples that God would keep them in spiritual unity and oneness in purpose and ministry. He noted that God had given Him these men whom He had trained to carry on His work. But Judas was "the son of perdition" or a product of eternal damnation (Ps. 109:7-8; Acts 1:20).

Jesus prayed not that God would take His followers *out* of the world but, rather, that He would keep them from the evil one. As they lived in the world as reflectors of the light of God's truth they would be hated, as He was hated. He then prayed that the Father would "sanctify" (v. 17) them through His truth. He knew that as they applied and obeyed the truth of God's Word, they would become different from the world. Then they would qualify to be "sent" into the world as ambassadors, just as Christ Himself was sent to represent the Father.

Christ prayed for His church (vv. 20-26).—In His omniscience, Jesus saw all who would believe and become a part of His Kingdom through the ministry of His disciples and all after them who would declare the gospel. His concern (v. 21) again was for unity. He linked the readiness of the world to believe on the testimony of the *unity* the world would see among believers. The "glory" (v. 22) Jesus gave His followers was the triumphant task of introducing people to God, which would become the focal point of their unity. This unity would be held together by the love of God given them and shared with one another and others.

Jesus then prayed for the maturity of His followers (v. 23), which would play a vital role in the effectiveness of their evangelistic ministry. He concluded His prayer with an expression of His longing to gather His own to Himself (v. 24) and with a desire to see the love of God in Him expressed in His followers, as He lived within them in the Person of the Holy Spirit.

A Prayer of Agony

Matthew 26:36-46

None of the recorded prayers of Jesus reveal the depth of His human agony as vividly as the prayer He prayed in the garden of Gethsemane. About three-fourths of a mile from the eastern wall of the ancient city of Jerusalem, across the Brook Kidron, is the garden of Gethsemane. Today, visitors are shown inside an enclosure about 200-feet square, adjacent to the beautiful Church of All Nations. Inside the enclosure are eight ancient, gnarled olive trees. Olive trees live for many hundreds of years. Some biblical historians believe one of these might well have been growing in the garden when Jesus prayed there.

The garden called Gethsemane (v. 36).—Gethsemane, to a student of the Scriptures, is not primarily a "place," but rather the supreme example of prayer in the life of Jesus. The word *Gethsemane* means "oil press" and indicates the owner of this grove of olive trees at one time may have been involved in producing olive oil, which had many uses in ancient Palestine. In Jesus' day it apparently was only a garden owned by someone whom Jesus knew and perhaps had ministered to. This friend of our Lord's obviously had made the garden available to Jesus and His disciples for a quiet place of retreat when they were in the Jerusalem area.

Probably it was about the midnight hour when Jesus and eleven of His disciples arrived at the entrance to the garden, after having spent the evening in an upper room in Jerusalem. There they had observed the Passover meal together, and Jesus had told them many things. He also had revealed His betrayer, and Judas had left the room to carry out his nefarious deed. Jesus told eight of the remaining eleven disciples who accompanied him to Gethsemane to remain outside the gate.

The desire for companionship in prayer (v. 37-38).—Jesus took Peter, James, and John a little farther inside the garden and asked them to wait for Him, probably suggesting, at least by inference, that they spend the time in prayer. These three men, representing Jesus' "inner circle," had been with Him at the transfiguration where they witnessed Moses and Elijah join Jesus in conversation about His approaching death. They also had accompanied Jesus inside Jairus's house where He raised the little girl from the dead. Jesus told them that His soul was "exceeding sorrowful, even unto death" (v. 38). The Man Jesus, who had never known sin, was experiencing the deepest anguish of His entire life. In fact, the agony He felt was severe enough to *kill* Him, were it not for the sustaining presence of His Heavenly Father. He knew that those three disciples could never enter into His sorrow in its fullness, but just to have them near and praying with Him would mean so much.

The depths of Jesus' spiritual suffering (v. 39).—When Jesus had prostrated Himself on the ground in heartrending prayer, He cried out, "O my Father, if it be possible, let this cup pass from me." Normally, when Jesus prayed, He said merely "Father." But under this extreme pressure, He cried "*my* Father," thus reaching up as closely as possible to

His Father's heart. The writer of Hebrews tells us that these words Jesus prayed were uttered with "strong crying and tears" (Heb. 5:7). The "Man" Jesus had to feel this total agony caused by His awareness of the approaching burden of the world's sins which was about to be thrust upon Him. The "cup" was a figurative expression of a bitter, deadly potion.

Jesus' words, "if it be possible," leaves the ultimate decision concerning His appeal up to the will and wisdom of His Father. If there was any other way to redeem the world without drinking that horrible cup, Jesus asked the Father to explore such a possibility. But quickly He added, "Nevertheless not as I will, but as thou wilt." Because of the sinless nature of our Lord, there was quick and unqualified acquiescence to the Father's will.

The disappointing disciples (vv. 40-41).—Jesus arose from His prone position and went to where the three disciples were waiting, and He found them asleep. Perhaps He sought to speak a word or two with them, to gain the human comfort that comes from understanding friends. The tragedy in this instance was that Jesus' closest friends did *not* understand. In all fairness, their sleeping must not be attributed solely to unconcern for their Master. The past days for them had been harrowing in many ways. Jesus had told them much during the past hours that they were *not* able to comprehend. In fact, "the spirit indeed is willing, but the flesh is weak" (v. 41).

The resolution of the agony (vv. 42-46).—Finding the disciples asleep and thus unaware of the battle He was fighting within His spirit, Jesus left them alone and returned to His private place of prayer. He continued praying His prayer to His Father until He had "prayed through" the matter. He submitted to His Father's will and surrendered Himself to be the acceptable Sacrifice for the sins of the world. Matthew noted that Jesus prayed "the third time, saying the same words" (v. 44). After Jesus' temptation in the wilderness following His baptism, Luke noted in his Gospel that Satan "departed from him for a season" (Luke 4:13). Could it be possible that this struggle our Lord encountered in Gethsemane was another temptation from Satan?

The revelation of the betrayal (vv. 45-46).—The battle was over. Jesus had submitted without reservation to His Father's will. He was committed to the cross, and perhaps it was at this point Jesus reached that moment described by the writer of Hebrews: "For the joy that was set before him [He] endured the cross, despising the shame" (Heb. 12:2).

Application

The three prayers of Jesus chosen for this study demonstrate in perfection how that the prayers and the life of a person are inseparably woven together. From the standpoint of human logic, many people wrestle with the concept of prayer. Some believe that because God is omniscient, it is somewhat presumptuous for us to "inform" Him in prayer concerning our needs or the needs of others. They also maintain that His total knowledge of us includes the effecting of His will and that the only prayer we need to pray is one affirming His will.

Of course, God *is* omniscient, and His will *is* incontestable. Yet communication with the Heavenly Father is vital, for not only does it establish an ongoing relationship, but it also plays an important role in a believer's understanding of personal need in the light of the working out of God's will. Thus, one's prayer life becomes the key to spiritual power. Jesus demonstrated this to His disciples when they had tried to heal the epileptic boy and had failed. When they asked Jesus why they had not been able to perform the healing, He explained to them, "This kind can come forth by nothing, but by prayer and fasting" (Mark 9:29). In that instance, prayer was the difference between success and failure.

Jesus also demonstrated in His prayer life that prayer provides fellowship with the Father. In a vivid and colorful way, Jesus compared the concern of the Heavenly Father for His children with that of an earthly father's determination to give good things to his children (Matt. 7:9-11). Jesus' prayer life revealed that He not only prayed during the great crises of His life, such as the prayer in Gethsemane, but also He prayed when there was no stated emergency or need that had arisen.

The first of the three prayers in this study is a Model Prayer Jesus gave His disciples to help them understand the constituent parts of a believer's prayer life. He did not mean, of course, that we must include all of these areas of need every time we pray. Rather, the petitions of the Model Prayer cover every part of a person's life. They deal with worship, petition, and praise.

The high priestly prayer in John 17 reveals the heart of Jesus in regard to His own personal relationship with His Father, His understanding of His mission, and His deep concern for His own. The prophetical nature of the prayer indicates that Jesus' intercessory ministry is continuing today as He fulfills His role as our great High Priest, seated at the right hand of the Father in heaven.

The prayer Jesus prayed in Gethsemane reflects the deep mystery of our Lord's sinless humanity struggling with the prospect of becoming sin for us in His death on the cross (2 Cor. 5:21). The lesson we can learn from that agonizing prayer is that God's will for our lives is always supreme, even though there are those instances when it involves that which is beyond our understanding. When we accept God's will for our lives, we experience peace even in the midst of conflict and crisis.

Outline: Prayers of Jesus

Introduction

The three prayers of Jesus chosen for this study reveal three facets of our Lord's life and ministry. The Model Prayer is a profoundly simple compilation of His teachings on prayer. The high priestly prayer in John 17 provides insight into the way Jesus conceived His own mission, and the prayer in Gethsemane demonstrated for eternity the significance of the will of God in the lives of His children.

A Model Prayer: Matthew 6:9-13

1. The "how" of prayer (v. 9a)
2. Our relationship to God and to His kingdom (vv. 9b-10)
3. Our relationship to ourselves, to our needs, and to others (vv. 11-13)

A Priestly Prayer: John 17

1. Christ prayed for Himself (vv. 1-5)
2. Christ prayed for His disciples (vv. 6-19)
3. Christ prayed for His church (vv. 20-26)

A Prayer of Agony: Matthew 26:36-46

1. The garden called Gethsemane (v. 36)
2. The desire for companionship in prayer (vv. 37-38)
3. The depths of Jesus' spiritual suffering (v. 39)
4. The disappointing disciples (vv. 40-41)
5. The resolution of the agony (vv. 42-46)

11 PRAYERS OF JAMES

Introduction

Three prominent men in the New Testament bear the name of James. Appearing first in the Scriptures is one of the original twelve disciples of Jesus. This James and his brother, John, were fishing partners with Simon Peter. They also are referred to as "sons of Zebedee."

Another of the twelve disciples was James the son of Alphaeus (Matt. 10:3). Some have held to the view that the mother of this James was a sister-in-law of Jesus' mother because of their marriage to two brothers: Cleophas and Joseph.

The James about whom we are concerned in this study, however, was a son of Mary and Joseph, and thus a stepbrother of Jesus, according to the natural interpretation of Matthew 13:55 and Mark 6:3. He was not one of the original twelve apostles of Jesus, nor was he even a believer in Jesus' messiahship at first (John 7:5). The narrative in the first chapter of Acts indicates that James and "his brethren" were with those who waited in the upper room in Jerusalem for the coming of the Holy Spirit (Acts 1:14). According to the apostle Paul, James was among those who saw the risen Christ during the period between the resurrection and ascension (1 Cor. 15:7). Like Paul and Barnabas, James received the title of apostle (Gal. 1:19). He was a leader in the church at Jerusalem and president of the first council (Acts 15:13). James, along with the elders of the Jerusalem church, received Paul upon his return from his third missionary journey (Acts 21:18). Eusebius noted in his writings that James was called "the Just" by his peers because of the eminent virtue of fairness he possessed.

Tradition holds that James was known as "Camel-knees" by the early Christians. Alexander Whyte wrote of him, "When they came to coffin him, it was like coffining the knees of a camel rather than the knees of a man, so hard, so worn, so stiff were they with prayer, and so unlike any other dead man's knees they had ever coffined."

Some Bible scholars have questioned the value of James's epistle. For most of his life, Martin Luther had little use for it, calling it "a strawy epistle." Yet the epistle contains the simple, straightforward teaching of Jesus. Along with other themes, James stressed the importance of prayer. There are no actual prayers in the epistle, yet there are specific instructions concerning the privilege and power of prayer.

In this chapter we will examine three specific instructions regarding prayer James set down for his readers in his epistle. The first, a prayer for wisdom, is concerned with the need for a believer to pray for wisdom in his life. The second study deals with unanswered prayers. James pointed out clearly why the prayers of believers are not answered. The third word about prayer we will explore is the need James expressed for prevailing prayer.

A Prayer for Wisdom

James 1:5-8,17

The dictionary's definition of wisdom leaves something to be desired in regard to the meaning of *spiritual* wisdom, to which James referred in this portion of his epistle. The dictionary states that wisdom is based on knowledge, experience, understanding, and so forth. From the standpoint of human wisdom, that may be true. But James had introduced his epistle by addressing the problem of trials and temptations that surrounded the first-century Christians to whom he was writing.

The problem of despair (v. 5).—The early believers faced great difficulty in practicing their faith and in maintaining their spiritual convictions. They were misunderstood, and because of the totally unique nature of the teachings of Christ by which they were trying to live, they often were considered enemies of the state. James was writing primarily to Christian Jews of the Diaspora, those who had been scattered abroad because of the great persecution of Christians. They were opposed not only by their own fellow Jews, but also by the pagan Romans who saw their zealous adherence to their faith as a threat to the *pax Romana*, the "Roman peace."

From every human standpoint, the outlook was bleak and the future uncertain. No doubt many of them were discouraged, and some may even have given way to self-pity in their despair. They did not need the speculative, theoretical wisdom of some system of philosophy. They needed a God-given understanding in the face of humanly mystifying circumstances.

James followed through on the inference that some of

them lacked the wisdom to handle their trials and troubles by stating that the wisdom they needed was not only available, but the One who could provide it was anxious to do so. If they would but *ask* God for this wisdom, not only in the instance of *one* trial but in the face of *every* dilemma that came to them, He would respond "liberally." There is nothing within the nature of God that keeps Him from giving, except our lack of faith in approaching Him with our needs. It is His practice to give generously.

Furthermore, God does not scold His children when they approach Him with their needs. He is not a begrudging Heavenly Father who berates His children when they come to Him with their requests. He understands fully our shortcomings, and loves us in spite of them.

The proper climate for prayer (v. 6).—Certainly there is nothing in God that would prevent Him from answering the prayers of His people for wisdom, but there could exist a barrier within the people *themselves*. When believers pray for wisdom to endure the trials of life, they must ask "in faith," or in connection with their faith. A Christian's prayer for wisdom must spring from a true faith in God and for the purpose of growing and developing in the faith as a result of the testing periods that come. When the prayer for wisdom is offered in this manner, the unqualified promise is that "it shall be given him"(v. 5). God desires to bring the faith of every believer to this ultimate goal of completeness. Furthermore, this asking "in faith" must be positive and conclusive, "nothing wavering." The indecision caused by doubt is the avowed enemy of faith.

The dilemma of the doubter (vv. 7-8).—James used a striking figure of speech in describing the doubting person. God sees such a person like a sea wave driven by the wind and tossed up and down. A wave of the sea is unstable. It is at the mercy of the wind, driven first this way, and then another.

In its tossing motion, it keeps going up and down; it is never stable and dependable. Thus, it runs in whatever direction the fickle wind carries it.

Doubting persons react spiritually in the same way. They turn this way and that, and they are "up and down" in their spiritual lives. There is little or no constancy in their experience, and they swing from enthusiasm to discouragement. These persons, stated James, need not expect to receive anything from the Lord. The wisdom needed in order to cope with trials and trouble would be ever beyond their reach.

The nature of that which comes from God (v. 17).—Nothing except that which is good and complete will come to God's children from their Heavenly Father. The reason why James could make this unqualified statement is because the God who is the Source of these blessings is One "with whom is no variableness, neither shadow of turning"(v. 17). James had described God as "the Father of lights." He was the Creator of those mystifying and indescribable heavenly bodies. But even those fabulous celestial creations vary in their light. Sometimes they are brighter than they are at other times. But they are only *creations* of this Almighty God. With Him, there is total, perfect, immutable constancy. There is never the hint of change. Thus it is from *this* God, who is our Heavenly Father, that the wisdom to understand life is offered to those who will ask for it.

Unanswered Prayers

James 4:2-3

One Bible commentator has noted, in regard to the kind of praying that is addressed in these two verses, that James was talking about "prayer that misses the target." The inference, of course, is that true, effective praying *always* has a goal—a target—that is provided by a need or by a relieved, difficult situation calling for gratitude. In other words, the motivation of genuine prayer is created either by a pressing emergency requiring intercession or else by the overflowing thanksgiving of the heart because of a thrilling answer to prayer. Even a prayer that seems pure adoration or worship is prompted by a realization of God's blessings and goodness and a natural desire to respond with gratitude.

Things that short-circuit prayer (v. 2.—James was not referring to literal war and bloodshed but to spiritual battles within the fellowship of believers that were even more vicious and destructive than physical conflicts. Though the power of the Holy Spirit was manifested in miraculous proportions in the early church in order to validate and establish it in those early, difficult days of its existence, the sinful human nature of believers still existed. Often there arose conflicts and crises within the congregations of believers. James did not elaborate on them except to infer that they were rooted in the lust for power, popularity, and authority on the part of certain members.

"Ye kill, and desire to have" was James's accusation. Instead of physical murder, James probably referred to the hatred Jesus described as being a parent to murder (Matt. 5:21-22). John also stated plainly that "whosoever hateth his brother is a murderer" (1 John 3:15). Human beings are total persons, and it is not possible to compartmentalize them so that what happens in the marketplace has no bearing or influence on what happens in the worship assembly, or vice versa. Genuine Christianity will permeate one's entire being, inspiring determination to practice Christ's principles of life even when doing so is not only unpopular but at times disastrously offensive. These first-century believers were doing exactly what twentieth-century Christians often do. Because of their lack of genuine commitment to Christ and to the living of His gospel, they were bringing into their worship assemblies on the Lord's Day the same unregenerate and unchristian attitudes they were practicing in the marketplace during the week.

The failure to ask (v. 2).—What these worldly-minded believers sought for in such unchristian ways obviously was not within the will and purpose of God for them. Consequently, they did not get what they wanted. Then, plainly, James said that "ye have not, because ye ask not."

Instead of praying, they were lusting and fighting. If they had genuinely sought God's will through earnest prayer, they would not have fallen victims to the unholy attitudes and actions James described. Sincere prayer not only establishes contact with God, it also serves as a purifying activity in which the presence of God's Spirit cleanses the soul of the one praying.

Asking for wrong things (v. 3).—If we expect God to answer our prayers, we must pray aright. In regard to our requests, God takes into account not only *what* we want but *why* we want it. Many things render our prayers inadmissible to God's ear. Certainly, unconfessed sin is an impenetrable barrier. The psalmist learned that lesson, for he wrote, "If I regard iniquity in my heart, the Lord will not hear me" (Ps. 66:18).

Unbelief is another hindrance to answered prayer. Sometimes our praying is perfunctory, a "going through the motions" activity. Perhaps this is what the writer of Hebrews had in mind when he said, "But without faith it is impossible to please him: for he that cometh to God must believe that he is, and that he is a rewarder of them that diligently seek him" (Heb. 11:6). Those who come "to God" must not only believe that He *is*, but that He is able to answer their prayers in accord with His will.

An unforgiving spirit harbored within one's heart makes

it impossible for God to hear and answer prayer. Jesus made this clear when He said, in the Sermon on the Mount, "Therefore if thou bring thy gift to the altar, and there rememberest that thy brother hath aught against thee; Leave there thy gift before the altar, and go thy way; first be reconciled to thy brother, and then come and offer thy gift" (Matt. 5:23-24).

The word *amiss* means "with wrong intent." As strange as it seems, we can ask God for good things with a wrong motive. In doing this, we are guilty of attempting to manipulate God, to make prayer an Aladdin's lamp or an instrument of *our* desires, rather than subjecting all of our desires to God. Unanswered prayers are not such because of God's reluctance to hear and bless us. Without exception, we will find upon honest investigation that our prayers go unanswered for negative reasons that lie within ourselves. Selfishness is a sinister and treacherous attitude that serves to paralyze a meaningful prayer life.

Prevailing Prayer

James 5:13-18

In these closing words of the epistle, James pours out an avalanche of words dealing with the power and scope of prayer. The reader gets the message immediately that prayer operates in *any* realm. These revelations from James's pen are all the more amazing in the light of the practicality of this venerable Christian leader. No one could say that James was guilty of a false mysticism in regard to the spiritual life. Whereas James's head may indeed have been "in the clouds" with spiritual ecstasy on occasion, still he had "both feet on the ground."

Prayer, the answer for distress (v. 13).—"Is any among you afflicted? Let him pray." "Afflicted" carries the idea here of being in trouble rather than suffering some physical malady. The early Christians were often in trouble because of their allegiance to Jesus Christ. Not only were they persecuted on religious grounds, they were discriminated against in their social relationships and their jobs. Their families suffered. Indeed, to many of the Christians in James's day, bad things were happening to good people. What were they to do? Were they to surrender to feelings of self-pity? Were they to adopt stoical attitudes in which they considered themselves the victims of a relentless and irreversible fate? James said that they were to *pray*. In so doing, they were to cast their heavy burdens and distresses upon the Lord. In such circumstances, God often answers by giving patience to bear it, not necessarily by alleviating the situation. And through the experience of learning patience, one grows stronger in one's Christian faith.

Prayer, the response to blessings (v. 13).—Then, in a rather strange combination of emotional reactions, James continued by asking, "Is any merry? Let him sing psalms." Perhaps what James was endeavoring to get across to his readers was that one must not come to God in prayer only when in distress but also in times of blessing. We do not find it difficult to think about praying when we are in trouble. But often we forget to pray when things are going well for us.

The word *merry* James used means more than to be outwardly happy, an emotion that is dependent upon circumstances. Rather the cheerfulness described here is an inner sense of well-being, whatever the prevailing conditions may be. Paradoxically, a Christian can be joyful even when surrounding circumstances are bad. The expression James used—"Let him sing psalms"—can mean either praise by means of a harp or a song sung to God with or without instrumental accompaniment.

Prayer, an opportunity to help others (v. 14).—Sickness, or "weakness" as the word is sometimes translated, is another instance in which prevailing prayer is needed. James has listed prayer as an antidote for the person in trouble, for one in good spirits, and now for one who is suffering physically. Often when persons are experiencing physical pain and discomfort, they find it extremely difficult to pray for themselves. The chronic pain often prohibits them from concentrating on communication with God and causes thoughts to be focused on the pain itself.

James suggested that this sufferer, who apparently was confined to the sick bed, should call for the "elders of the church" and ask them to come and "pray over him." The elders in the early church usually were older men who had sufficient experience and ability to teach and guide the congregations of believers. This arrangement was taken from the synagogue, and they functioned somewhat as modern-day pastors do, although there was more than one in a congregation.

There are two opinions in regard to "anointing him with oil." Some believe it was a symbolic act with the oil representing the Holy Spirit, through whose power healing can be effected. We know that oil was one of the most common medicines of biblical times. The Samaritan in Jesus' story poured "in oil and wine" in his first-aid ministry to the wounded man (Luke 10:34). On this basis, some interpret James to be prescribing prayer and medicine in the case of the person who is ill. Certainly, God is able to heal without medical assistance. But who can question the divine blessing of medical discoveries that have cured the sick person of his disease or physical malady, or at least dramatically improved the quality of life of the sufferer?

Prayer, a ministry of salvation (v. 15).—If there is any question about any mystic qualities resident in the anointing oil, this statement James made should provide the answer. That which ultimately restores the sick person is "the prayer of faith," and the One who raises him up is "the Lord." Furthermore, there is a *spiritual* healing that accompanies the physical restoration. The spiritual deformity caused by unconfessed and unforgiven sin is even more serious than the physical problem. The conditional clause beginning with "if" disclaims the ancient belief that *all* suffering was the result of personal sin. James's statement left open the possibility that we *do* bring some of our problems upon ourselves because of our sins. But not all suffering can be related to a personal and deliberate breaking of God's laws.

The basis for effective and fervent prayer (vv. 16-18).—In the preceding verse, James connected confession of sin with the prayer of faith. Here he followed through by stating that there are times when Christians need to confess their sins to each other. Note that it was not just the elders who were to pray but *all* believers. If a Christian has consciously sinned against another person, he or she should not rest until the wrong is righted.

Then, when the "air is cleared" and a right relationship is established both with God and with one's fellow believer, one's praying will avail "much." A "righteous" person is one who is right with God because sin has been confessed. This role is not reserved for the spiritually elite but for *any* believer who is right with God.

Then, to illustrate his point, James mentioned Elijah's experience with the drought in Israel. James was careful to point out that Elijah was "a man subject to like passions as we are." God used him as a channel through whom to demonstrate His power before His people. They had sinned, and the judgment was that there would be no rain. For three-and-a-half years the drought persisted. Then, because

Elijah was "right with God," he prayed, and God answered and sent rain to end the drought. The point James was making is that *anyone* who is right with God can pray within God's will, and his prayer will be powerful and effective. Elijah, though he was a man just like us and had no superhuman powers, was in a position to be used of God. Prevailing prayer, whether from one who is in trouble or in good spirits or physically ill or at odds with a brother or sister, is dependent upon one's standing with God.

Application

The fact that James may have been the first "pastor" of the Jerusalem church, as we conceive the role, leads us to understand why he had so much to say about prayer. The distance of the years often adds a dimension of unrealistic glamour to history. We read of the miracle-studded experiences of the early church—the amazing healings, those raised from the dead—and we think, *How great it would have been to have lived and worshiped in one of those first-century congregations!* But one has only to read the Book of Acts and the Epistles of Paul to realize that the problems in the first-century church were overwhelming.

Because of that, James surely was driven often to prayer. When he dealt with the prayer for wisdom, he doubtlessly spoke from experience. For not only he, but many of his people suffered trials and heartaches which seemed terribly unjust and unfair. Probably some doubted if God was even aware of the plight they were in. James knew they would need divine wisdom to accept, if not understand, much that was happening to them.

Christians in every era suffer those life-shattering calamities that defy understanding. Often we find ourselves facing head-on some storm of life for which there is neither rhyme nor reason. When we try futilely to ferret out the reasons for what is happening to us or to our loved ones, we encounter the proverbial brick wall. James's advice is pertinent for us. If we ask God, He will give us wisdom to accept, with patience, what is taking place, even if we cannot understand it.

We often have difficulty believing that the early Christians could be guilty of those sins of the spirit James named in chapter 4 of his epistle which would hinder their prayer lives. And yet they were subject to the same temptations to sin that we are. They were victims of hatred and covetousness, attitudinal sins that destroyed the effectiveness of their praying. When we feel heaven is a wall that our prayers slam against, and then fall back in our faces, we would do well to examine our own hearts and our attitudes toward others. Also, the motivation behind our praying plays a major role in answered prayer.

As James brought the epistle to a close, he seems to have tried to crowd in everything he could on the subject of prayer. He literally "covered the waterfront" in dealing with the major areas where prayer is a must in a believer's life. He began with those in trouble. Instead of feeling sorry for themselves, they should pray. Probably the hardest time for us to pray is when suffering some setback that we feel is totally unjust. Usually we tend to want to retreat and lick our wounds and blame God or someone else for our bad times.

Then there are times when good things happen to us. Perhaps the answer to a prayer that we have prayed repeatedly for years has come. The tendency is to "relax" in the intensity of our praying. James said that "good times" provide excellent opportunities to offer prayers of praise and thanksgiving to God. We do very little of this, anyway. Most of our praying is petitionary. We are moved to pray far more often when we are in trouble than when we are in the midst of blessing.

Joining together in prayer for the sick is another area that is sometimes neglected. Suffering persons often are in such a state that they find it impossible to intercede for themselves. In fact, the nature of their illness may be of such a critical nature that they *cannot* pray for themselves. To join together in prayer for a brother or sister in Christ demonstrates a function of the body of Christ that is commendable indeed.

James concluded his epistle, in which he had dealt so extensively with prayer, by reminding his readers that effective, powerful prayer experiences were not the privilege of certain special persons in God's family. Any person who is right with God can become a channel through whom the divine power can function. Effective prayer surely is an untapped reservoir of untold blessings within the church.

Outline: Prayers of James

Introduction

The three areas of prayer chosen for this study represent the broad treatment James gave to the subject of prayer in his brief epistle. The first prayer, "A Prayer for Wisdom," deals with divine wisdom to understand the trials and temptations that come in Christians' lives. "Unanswered Prayers" provides a straightforward explanation of the sins of the spirit that can destroy a believer's prayer life. Thirdly, "Prevailing Prayer" touches upon several diverse areas in which prayer can change one's life and affect the lives of others.

A Prayer for Wisdom: James 1:5-8,17

1. The problem of despair (v. 5)
2. The proper climate for prayer (v. 6)
3. The dilemma of the doubter (vv. 7-8)
4. The nature of that which comes from God (v. 17)

Unanswered Prayers: James 4:2-3

1. Things that short-circuit prayer (v. 2)
2. The failure to ask (v. 2)
3. Asking for wrong things (v. 3)

Prevailing Prayer: James 5:13-18

1. Prayer, the answer for distress (v. 13)
2. Prayer, the response to blessings (v. 13)
3. Prayer, an opportunity to help others (v. 14)
4. Prayer, a ministry of salvation (v. 15)
5. The basis for effective and fervent prayer (vv. 16-18)

■ 12 PRAYERS IN THE REVELATION

Introduction

Up to this point in our study of "Great Prayers of the Bible," we have focused on individuals in both Old and New Testaments in whose lives prayer played a major role. In the last two chapters we will examine prayers offered by groups of believers who communicated with God in the midst of varying circumstances. As we have noted in the previous studies, the basic needs of people have not changed, whether they lived in the days of Moses and the patriarchs, in the time of Christ, or today. Thus all of these prayers have a universal and timeless relevance to human needs.

The three prayers we will examine in this chapter are found in the Book of Revelation. People tend to approach any study from the Revelation with mixed feelings. Some feel the subject matter in this apocalyptic book is so cryptic and potentially confusing that they avoid it altogether. At the other extreme, there are those who become so obsessed and fascinated with the futuristic contents of the Revelation that they neglect other portions of the Bible and spend the majority of their time studying and trying to decipher the detailed plan of God for the end of time.

Yet in between these two extreme approaches, there can be found golden spiritual nuggets and valuable, applicable truths for our lives today. Such is the case with the three prayers chosen for this particular study.

An important consideration is this: what is recorded in Revelation are the contents of a vision God gave to John while he was in exile on the Isle of Patmos. Through His Spirit, God enabled John to observe events that were going to come to pass before the end of time, and also after time has been declared to be no more. Herschel Hobbs entitled his book on Revelation, *The Cosmic Drama*, an apt description of the revelation John received. For John saw enacted before Him scenes of such awesome and inexpressible magnitude that he struggled with the limitations of his own vocabulary to record them.

A thrilling discovery in the midst of this oft-times perplexing Book is the fact that *prayer* played a prominent role. Even in those settings in which John saw the people of God in heaven, in the very presence of the Almighty God, the people prayed. In these three prayers chosen for this study, we will discover the essence of praise and adoration, along with a petition for the glorious consummation of God's eternal plan of the ages.

A Prayer of Praise to the Lamb

Revelation 5:9-10

This vision John saw was overwhelming in its magnitude, for not only did the heavens reverberate with the sound of this majestic hymn-prayer of praise to the Lamb of God, but also the prayer commemorated the coming forth of the Lamb to open the seven-sealed book. This mysterious book that John saw "in the right hand of him that sat on the throne" (5:1) contained the prophecy of events yet to come, including both the salvation of God's people and the judgment of the wicked. In other words, it was the "authorized record" of God's redemptive plan for the conclusion of human history, the overthrow of evil, and the gathering of God's redeemed people to enjoy for eternity the blessings of God's righteous rule.

When the first call was issued for one to step forward and take the book from the hand of God, open its seals, and reveal its contents, no one responded. The prospect of having the contents of the book forever hidden was a devastating thought to John, so much so that he "wept much" (v. 4). This period of anxious waiting for John only served to heighten his anticipation of the resolution of this crisis.

Then the main character in this magnificent drama stepped forth, and he "stood a Lamb as it had been slain" (v. 6). The metaphor of the lamb was the central figure of Isaiah's great prophecy of the Suffering Servant (Isa. 53). When He took the book, even before a single seal was opened or a word concerning its contents was revealed, "the four beasts and four and twenty elders fell down before the Lamb, . . . And they sang a new song" (v. 8). The majesty of the Lamb of God was such that instant assurance came to the heavenly observers, and their hearts overflowed with this hymn-prayer of praise to God.

This brief prayer has a contrapuntal character in that three basic declarations are woven together to produce its theme. In music, "counterpoint" is the fusing of two or more independent melodies that, according to the fixed rules of harmony, interact with and thus complement each other. These three themes or "melody lines" deal with redemption, royalty, and consecration.

The new song (v. 9).—John was careful to note that the song they sang was a "new song." Often in Old Testament worship, the people were told to sing unto the Lord a new song (Ps. 33:3; 98:1; 144:9; 149:1). The designation "a new song" did not describe a song that had not been sung before, but, rather, it indicated a fresh song of praise. But the phrase also could mean a special song composed for some great occasion. Such would be the nature of this "new song" about to be sung in heaven. The new redeemed order of God's kingdom was about to be introduced. The word *new* appears significantly in Revelation, making it a book that is characterized by new things. There is a new name for the redeemed (2:17; 3:12); the new Jerusalem (3:12; 21:2); new heavens and a new earth (21:1); and all things made new (21:5).

The theme of redemption (v. 9).—The prayer began with a positive statement of fact: "Thou art worthy to take the book" (v. 9). The worthiness of the Lamb "as it had been slain" (v. 6) was established not because of His deity, His incarnation, His sinless human life, or His relation to God but because of the redemption provided by His death on the cross.

"For thou wast slain, and hast redeemed us to God by thy blood" (v. 9). This expression is rooted in the ancient practice of a slave buying freedom from bondage by offering a sum of money. The slave would deposit the money in a temple with the belief that the god of that temple would in turn purchase the slave from a human owner. Thus, the former owner of the slave would receive the money from the temple, and the slave would receive freedom. Actually, in the pagan ceremony, the slave remained the property of the god.

When a person is redeemed and becomes a member of the family of God, the transaction takes place because Christ purchased that individual from the bondage of sin and death "for God." The price of the purchase was Christ's blood. Every believer in the Lord Jesus Christ is the purchased possession of God, for we are "bought with a price" (1

Cor. 6:20). Thus the theme of redemption becomes the major melody line in this hymn-prayer, forming the basis for its contents.

The theme of royalty (v. 10).—The second theme or melody line which is woven into this prayer is stated, "[Thou] hast made us unto our God kings" (v. 10). Most translators agree that "kings" is better rendered "kingdom" (v. 10, NIV). The concept of a kingdom was predominant in both Old and New Testaments. The people of Israel had wanted a king in the beginning because all of the other nations around them had kings. God permitted that arrangement, and Saul became Israel's first king. Only two more kings, David and Solomon, reigned over the united kingdom. When the kingdom divided into Israel and Judah, however, there followed a succession of kings. A few were strong and righteous, but most were weak and evil. Yet because the people understood kings, kingdoms, and royalty, Jesus used that analogy in characterizing Himself as a King and His followers as His subjects, or members of His kingdom. Those of us who are conditioned to a republic, and know nothing of life under the absolute rule of a king or queen, cannot appreciate the full impact of this analogy. The ultimate import of the concept of a king and a kingdom, of course, is that of absolute sovereignty on the part of the king and unquestioning submission on the part of his subjects. When the King is a righteous and holy God, then there is joy and delight in submitting, without reservation, to His rule.

The theme of consecration (v. 10).—"[Thou] hast made us unto our God kings and priests." This statement concerning the priesthood of God's people in heaven is repeated later: "Blessed and holy is he that hath part in the first resurrection: on such the second death hath no power, but they shall be priests of God and of Christ, and shall reign with him a thousand years" (20:6). Priesthood is synonymous with a unique consecration to God, providing full and immediate access into His presence for the purpose of worshiping and praising Him.

Another unique feature of this heavenly relationship between God and His people is that they "shall reign on the earth" (v. 10). The redeemed will not only be a people over whom God reigns, but they also will be granted the privilege of sharing in His reign. Jesus had said during His Sermon on the Mount that the meek would "inherit the earth" (Matt. 5:5). The apostle Paul also stated that one day the saints of God would reign with Him (2 Tim. 2:12).

Therefore, this delightful prayer of praise and adoration to the Lamb combines the thrilling themes of God's plan of redemption and His magnanimous provision for His people to function as priests in His presence and to reign with Him as members of heavenly royalty.

A Prayer of the Glorified Saints

Revelation 19:1-10

The first ten verses of Revelation 19 contain another hymn-prayer from a great multitude in heaven who apparently are the assembled saints of God in glory. It is a song of salvation which focuses on praise to God for the triumph of His justice and the judgment which inevitably must accompany that justice.

A song about God's salvation (vv. 1-5).—John, the privileged observer of this celestial scene, heard the word *alleluia* as the first expression of praise from this throng. "Alleluia" is a transliteration of the Hebrew *haleel,* which means "praise Yahweh [God]." Interestingly, when this word appears in the Old Testament, it is translated "Praise the Lord." It is found transliterated as "alleluia" ("hallelujah,"

RSV) only in the Book of Revelation.

The affirmation of praise from the redeemed and glorified saints is that salvation, glory, and power all belong to God. Furthermore, they are careful to praise God for triumphing over evil. This grappling with evil is a necessary part of the salvation process. If there is not a judgment pronounced upon evil, then there is no effective standard against which sinful humans can measure themselves. Until there is a felt sense of guilt and need for forgiveness, then there can only be indifference toward God's offer of salvation. But God is not indifferent to evil, whether it is expressed in human suffering, in tyranny, or in idolatry. The holiness of God makes it imperative for Him to pass judgment upon evil. Thus, the jubilant praise to God from this throng is because truth has prevailed over wickedness.

The marriage of the Lamb (vv. 6-10).—There is a decided change of theme and atmosphere in the second half of the prayer-hymn. Again the prayer begins with "Alleluia," and it is a marvelous ascription of praise having to do with the marriage of the Lamb and the bride, His church. Both Old and New Testaments use this image for the church as a bride, which, in the New Testament, represents the perfect union of Christ and His church. Because of the imperfection of human nature, spiritual perfection cannot be experienced on earth. This barrier prevents us from enjoying the ultimate fullness of joy in Christ that awaits us in eternity.

Note also that Christ's bride "has made herself ready" (v. 7, RSV). The apostle Paul dealt with the preparation of the bride for marriage as an act of Christ accomplished by the giving of His life (Eph. 5:25). But here the implication is that the *bride* has made her own preparation. The fact is that whereas redemption is completely the work of God in Christ, there must be a human response. The apostle John wrote, "Beloved, now are we the sons of God, and it doth not yet appear what we shall be: but we know that, when he shall appear, we shall be like him; for we shall see him as he is. And every man that hath this hope in him purifieth himself, even as he is pure" (1 John 3:2-3).

In his great joy at this prospect, John fell down to worship the angel who interpreted this prayer of the glorified saints to him. But the angel refused to allow John to worship him, stating plainly, "See thou do it not: I am thy fellowservant, and of thy brethren that have the testimony of Jesus: worship God" (v. 10).

Thus, in this exciting prayer of praise containing its four "alleluias" there is the promise of the vindication of God's moral order, the indisputable triumph of the kingdom of God, and of the ultimate purification of Christ's church in heaven.

A Prayer of Consummation

Revelation 22:17,20

This incomparable vision or revelation that God gave to John on Patmos reaches a glorious climax in its final chapter. We might compare this chapter to the great finale of a symphonic work. The theme of the symphony has been woven by the composer in and out of the various movements, with all of the countermelodies, the trills and flourishes of the flutes and piccolos, the arresting tones of the trumpets, and the delicate flow of the strings. Now the time has come for the percussion section of the orchestra to be heard. There are drum rolls, followed by the crystal-clear tones of the glockenspiel, and punctuated by the crashing of the cymbals. With that majestic introduction came a prayer from three sources: the Holy Spirit, the bride (the church), and John.

The prayer of the Spirit (v. 17).—The only recorded prayer of the Holy Spirit in the Bible occurs here, and, combined with the prayer of the church, it consists of a single word addressed to Christ, "Come." Three times in this chapter Jesus had promised, "I come quickly." Now the prayer of the Holy Spirit and of the church is that Jesus keep His promise and come.

We know that the Holy Spirit prays, for the apostle Paul indicated that there are times when believers are unable to pray with knowledge and discernment, and on such occasions the Holy Spirit will pray for and through us (Rom. 8:26). This prayer of the Spirit for Christ to "come," however, is unique. Jesus had stated clearly to His disciples the primary purpose of the Holy Spirit when He came: "He shall glorify me: for he shall receive of mine, and shall show it unto you" (John 16:14). A major ministry of the Holy Spirit in the world is to reveal the Lord Jesus more and more fully to those who have received Him as Savior. In His ministry to Christians, the Holy Spirit is constantly about the business of helping them grow "in grace, and in the knowledge of our Lord and Savior Jesus Christ" (2 Pet. 3:18). When Christ comes, of course, then the spiritual growth process shall have been completed, and this part of the Spirit's ministry will be finished.

The prayer of the church (v. 17).—The appeal of the Spirit is joined to that of the church in a combined cry to the Lord Jesus to "Come." When Jesus ascended back to the Father from the summit of the Mount of Olives, the angels reminded the disciples who stood looking after the disappearing Christ, "Ye men of Galilee, why stand ye gazing up into heaven? this same Jesus, which is taken up from you into heaven, shall so come in like manner as ye have seen him go into heaven" (Acts 1:11).

Through the long years, the church has awaited the return of Christ. Repeatedly through the Scriptures, the reminder is that He can come at any time. The apostle Paul even pronounced a blessing upon those who "love his appearing," or who anticipate with joy the return of Christ. They will receive "a crown of righteousness" (2 Tim. 4:8). Every generation of believers since the Day of Pentecost has experienced dark days of persecution and misunderstanding, and some have felt for certain that the time for Christ's coming was imminent. Yet Jesus told His disciples that no one knew the day nor the hour, and we were not to be concerned with the chronology of His coming but with preparation for that blessed event.

The statement "Let him that heareth say, Come" (v. 17) appears to be addressed historically to the members of the local congregations in John's time who were the first to receive this Revelation. They, too, were urged to join in the invitation of the Spirit and the church as a whole for Christ to return.

The first two sentences in this verse do *not* comprise an evangelistic appeal, but they reflect the yearning of the Spirit and the church for Christ to come. The third and fourth sentences represent an invitation to those who are *not yet* followers of Jesus to come and receive the free gift of the water of life. Thus, to the very end of the Bible, an appeal is offered to those who will to receive Christ.

The prayer of John (v. 20).—In reply to the threefold invitation to Jesus that He "come" and establish His kingdom on earth, thus ending the rule of evil forever, the Lord Jesus said, "Surely I come quickly. Amen." There will be no warning, no hesitation when He comes. The period of longsuffering and divine patience will be over.

Then, almost as a sigh and an echo, John prayed, "Even so, come, Lord Jesus." John's soul was filled to overflowing with all that he had witnessed throughout this magnificent vision. The culmination of it all was the coming of the Lord Jesus. In view of the awful judgment that was destined to come upon the rejecting world, John longed for the coming of his Lord to bring peace and righteousness upon the earth.

Verse 20 surely is one of the most remarkable verses in the Bible, for within its sixteen words it encompasses the last *promise* of the Bible ("Surely I come quickly") and the last *prayer* of the Bible ("Even so, come, Lord Jesus"). Coupled with John's concluding wish that "The grace of our Lord Jesus Christ be with you all" in verse 21, we have a thrilling end to a glorious Revelation.

Application

With few exceptions, most of the prayers recorded in Revelation follow the same theme of praise and adoration to God and to the Lamb, the crucified, risen, and glorified Son of God. This is true because the location of those who offer the prayers is in heaven, a place of perfection, fulfillment, and consummation. Those who at last bask in the celestial glory of God's presence will find that expressions of praise to God for His greatness and His grace in providing salvation for sinful human beings are ongoing expressions of eternal life.

The three prayers chosen for this portion of our study have praise and worship as their underlying theme, although the third of the trio is also a prayer of petition. Our prayers on this earth cannot contain the dimension of understanding and fullness that characterize these prayers, of course. We yet "see through a glass, darkly," and we only "know in part" (1 Cor. 13:12). But we anticipate that moment of fulfillment when "that which is perfect is come" (1 Cor. 13:10), and our prayers will be prayed with complete knowledge and understanding.

The first prayer, "A Prayer of Praise to the Lamb" (Rev.

5:9-10), contains not only the thrilling note of adoration expressed to Jesus, the Lamb of God, but also there is a sense of relief and satisfaction that a hopeless situation has been remedied. Often we experience something similar to this. We face a seemingly impossible and irreversible problem. Every avenue of hope for a solution apparently has been explored and abandoned. We are at the point of utter despair when, as if by a miracle, the answer materializes before us. Almost always it comes from an entirely unexpected source, and perhaps in a most unusual way. Then our prayer of thanksgiving and praise is a mixture of self-rebuke for our lack of belief and trust in God and overflowing gratitude to a loving and caring Heavenly Father. This was much the feeling in this particular prayer of praise. It seemed, for a while, that the book in God's hands would remain sealed, with its contents hidden forever. And yet, at the last, shining moment, the Lamb stepped forward and saved the day!

The second prayer, "A Prayer of the Glorified Saints" (Rev. 19:1-10), is punctuated with that universal word of praise, "Alleluia," appearing only here in the Scriptures. The prayer coming from the multitude of glorified saints combines three great expressions of the Almighty God which He has graciously extended toward sinful, undeserving people: salvation, glory, and power. Christians should never cease praising God for this great salvation provided freely for those who will receive it through repentance of sin and faith in the Lord Jesus Christ. Its greatness lies in its incalculable cost, the blood of the sinless Son of God, and in the fact it is a free gift to those who will accept God's offer.

No one can adequately define or explain the glory of God in human terms. *Glory* is one of those descriptive words in our vocabulary that truly has no limiting boundaries, except those we impose upon it because of our humanity. God's glory, His ineffable majesty, can only be absorbed in this life "in bits and pieces." In heaven we shall be able to bask for eternity in the fullness of God's glory and still never exhaust that which comprises its essence. Then, God's power also is boundless and matchless in its awesomeness. It has no equal, and there is no area of God's creation that is not touched and controlled through His divine power. In no other prayer in Revelation is there implied a more complete expression of God's being than in this one.

The final prayer of the three in this chapter, "A Prayer of Consummation" (Rev. 22:17,20), is unique in that it is an intense appeal to Christ from the Spirit, the church, and from John himself that Christ keep His promise and return to earth to rule and reign in His kingdom of righteousness. The promised return of Christ in the Scriptures often is either taken for granted by most Christians, or else it is relegated to some far-off, unreal time in a fantasy world. Yet there is no promise in the Bible more clearly given than the one that Christ will return. He was straightforward with His disciples about this. Furthermore, it is the one, redeeming hope for a world that continues, generation after generation, to experience deteriorating morals and an increasing denial of the reality of God's involvement in human affairs. For the Christian, the anticipated return of Christ is the one, shining light on the horizon of life.

Outline: Prayers in the Revelation

Praise and adoration, coupled with a plea for Christ to come and establish His kingdom as He had promised He would do, is the multifaceted theme of the three prayers in this study. The uniqueness of the prayers recorded in the revelation John received on Patmos is that they are couched in the perfect state and atmosphere of heaven, and are free of the limitations and imperfections that characterize earthly prayers.

A Prayer of Praise to the Lamb: Revelation 5:9-10

1. The new song (v. 9)
2. The theme of redemption (v. 9)
3. The theme of royalty (v. 10)
4. The theme of consecration (v. 10)

A Prayer of the Glorified Saints: Revelation 19:1-10

1. A song about God's salvation (vv. 1-5)
2. The marriage of the Lamb (vv. 6-10)

A Prayer of Consummation: Revelation 22:17,20

1. The prayer of the Spirit (v. 17)
2. The prayer of the church (v. 17)
3. The prayer of John (v. 20)

13 PRAYERS OF THE EARLY CHURCH

Introduction

Without the vital presence of the Holy Spirit indwelling the believers, the early church could not have survived. Every conceivable obstacle stood between the church and its success as an earthly institution. The forces of evil revealed themselves at every turn, beginning with the pagan environment of the Roman occupation of Palestine coupled with the ever-present hostility of the unbelieving Jewish leaders.

For a long time, the followers of Christ were considered only a dissident group within Judaism, a prickly thorn in the side of the Jewish hierarchy. For these Jewish Christians continued to worship in the Temple, observing the daily times of prayer. Many of them likely participated in the traditional feast weeks and religious celebrations that were so much a part of their heritage. Consequently, they were constantly being watched by the religious leaders at the Temple, and soon resentment by religious leaders expressed itself in increasingly severe acts of discrimination and persecution aimed at the ultimate destruction of the Christian movement.

In addition, normal problems began to develop within the fellowship of believers. In the Jerusalem church, there were few Gentile believers at the beginning, and among the Jewish Christians, there was conflict between Hellenistic Jews and Judean Jews. The Hellenistic Jews, those who lived in other parts of the Mediterranean world and spoke Greek, were not always held in the highest regard by the Judean Jews. These Judeans who had been born in Palestine and had lived there all of their lives rebelled at the Grecian language and customs of their fellow Jews who had come from other lands. The Jerusalem church sought to help widows within their fellowship, and soon the Hellenistic Jewish widows were complaining that they were being unfairly treated in deference to the Judean widows. As a result, seven men were appointed to relieve the apostles of this burdensome problem of equitable distribution (Acts 6:1-7).

In spite of these nagging problems that were constantly arising within the church, the fellowship of believers continued to grow, and with the growth came increasing persecution from without. This persecution, however, only served to deepen the commitment of the believers and to force them to depend more and more on God. As a result, they were driven to prayer, and, increasingly, they witnessed the miraculous movement of God among them in answer to their prayers.

After Jesus ascended into heaven and was no longer visibly present, His followers discovered a new relationship with Him. While He had been on earth, they had known Him as a Friend and Teacher. They had depended exclusively upon His physical presence among them. They had spoken with him face-to-face. But now, with the presence of the Holy Spirit who had come to indwell them on the Day of Pentecost, they would know Him as Lord and Savior. They would be aware of His presence as an unseen Friend in heaven. A new medium of communication with Him would develop as they spoke with Him in prayer. While He was on earth, they functioned only as His followers and learners.

Now a new dimension would be added to that relationship. They would also be His ambassadors and witnesses, teaching others about Him.

Yet the continuing focal point of their spiritual victory would lie in the exercise of the privilege of prayer. In this chapter, we will examine three specific examples of the effect of their praying. The first instance of prayer was implied as the 120 followers of Christ obeyed His command to wait in Jerusalem "for the promise of the Father" (Acts 1:4). Then, the moving prayer of Stephen on the occasion of his martyrdom was a shining example of an unshakable faith, and the corporate experience of prayer among the believers was demonstrated in their intercession for the release of the imprisoned Peter. In our study of these particular prayers, we will discover not only increasing awareness by the early Christians of the power of prayer, but also we will see how vital prayer is to the spiritual growth and development of every believer in the Lord Jesus Christ.

A Prayer of Preparation

Acts 1:4, 14

The stunned disciples stood on the Mount of Olives and watched Jesus ascend into heaven. Even though He had told them that He must return to His Father in heaven, and that He would send them "another Comforter" (John 14:16), they still could hardly imagine life without His physical presence. The angels had appeared to remind them that Jesus would come again as He had promised (John 14:3). Apparently the angel's words had jarred the disciples from their trancelike state of bewilderment, and they left the Mount of Olives and returned to Jerusalem.

Waiting for the promise (v. 4).—During one of His last postresurrection appearances, Jesus had told His disciples not to leave Jerusalem but to "wait for the promise of the Father." Jesus probably knew that the disciples were already thinking of returning to Galilee, their old home territory. That would be the natural thing to do, of course, for most of them probably had families still living in Galilee, and they would need to resume their work to provide for them.

In his Gospel, Luke recorded Jesus' words to His disciples regarding what they were to do after His ascension: "Behold, I send the promise of my Father upon you: but tarry ye in the city of Jerusalem, until ye be endued with power from on high" (Luke 24:49). This command of Jesus would coincide with the Acts record of His instructions to them to "wait" in Jerusalem. We do not know all that the followers of Christ did during that waiting period. They knew the Lord's promise that He would send "another Comforter." But they did not know all that He had meant by those words, except they were convinced they must obey His command. It was important for them to learn obedience and patience, for without those there would have been no Pentecostal experience for them. Without Pentecost, there would have been no church to evangelize the first-century world.

For ten days, the believers came daily to the Jerusalem meeting place. Apparently there was no program planned, and no activities to help them pass the time. They had no idea how long the waiting period would be—whether it would be for a day, a month, or a year. Nor did they have the slightest clue as to how this "promise of the Father" would manifest itself. Yet, in His sovereign wisdom, God was using this period of waiting in an effective and creative way among them.

A singleness of purpose (v. 14).—"These all continued with one accord." Where the believers assembled in Jerusalem is not indicated. Some believe that the room where they met was the same location where Jesus and His disciples observed the Passover meal on the night before His crucifixion. Others have suggested that they were meeting in a compartment of the Temple, basing their contention on the statement in Luke 24:53: "[They] were continually in the temple, praising and blessing God." On the other hand, upper rooms of private homes often were used for religious purposes. Many think they were meeting in the home of the disciple Mary, the mother of John Mark, where Christian disciples later assembled for prayer (Acts 12:12-16). A private dwelling like this would seem to be a more likely place for a group of this size to meet regularly for ten days than a room in the Temple. Also, the coming of the Holy Spirit is described as filling "all the house where they were sitting" (Acts 2:2).

Who were those who made up this assembly of 120 believers? Luke was careful to name the eleven disciples (v. 13), along with "the women, and Mary the mother of Jesus, and with his brethren" (v. 14). "The women" probably included those who were at the cross when Christ was crucified and also were present at the Resurrection. Among them would have been Mary Magdalene, from whom Christ had cast seven demons, and likely the wives of some of the apostles. The group of women probably would have included also the wives and relatives of other devout followers of Christ. We can imagine that Joanna, the wife of Herod's steward, along with Susanna and other women who had been healed of illnesses or demon possession were there (Luke 8:2-3). And we would not omit Mary, the mother of James and Joses; Salome, the wife of Zebedee (Mark 15:40); Mary and Martha of Bethany, and certainly John Mark's mother, Mary, who may have been hostess to the company of believers. With the disciples and the women, there were Jesus' brothers. This is somewhat surprising, for Jesus' brothers in Nazareth had not believed in Him (John 7:5). Yet after His resurrection, Jesus had appeared specifically to James (1 Cor. 15:7), who is generally believed to have been the Lord's brother and the one who became leader of the church in Jerusalem (Acts 12:17; 15:13; 21:18). Most evangelical Bible authorities believe that these were the sons of Mary and Joseph and thus stepbrothers of Jesus. In all, the total assembly amounted to 120 persons (v. 15).

In spite of the diversity of those present, there was an amazing unity of spirit and purpose. Luke recorded that they were of "one accord," or with one mind. Unity was the cohesive, spiritual climate in that upper room. They were united in their determination to obey the command of their Lord to assemble in Jerusalem and wait. They also were united in the purpose of their assembling together, which was to "wait for the promise of the Father." Then, obviously, they were united in their resolve to continue meeting and waiting as long as necessary.

Faithfulness in prayer (v. 14).—Interestingly, this event marked the first recorded prayer meeting of the early church, and it lasted ten days! Historically, the church was born in a prayer meeting, and experience has indicated that the life and effectiveness of the church's ministry has continued to depend upon a consistent atmosphere of prayer.

But what was the nature of their praying? Though we are not told what they prayed about, we can surmise that they were preparing themselves for the coming of the Holy Spirit by searching their own hearts and confessing their sins and shortcomings both to God and to each other. At this point they probably were not able to conceive the magnitude of the task that lay ahead of them as being channels through whom God would extend His offer of salvation to a lost world. No doubt they knew something great and earth-shattering was about to take place, for they were still ecstatic because of the reality of the risen Christ. He had kept His promise to rise from the dead. Now they had no reason to doubt but that He would also keep His promise to send the other "Comforter," who would abide not only *with* them but *within* them.

A Prayer of a Martyr

Acts 7:54-60

There are no isolated events in the lives of God's people as they relate to each other and to God's plan for the salvation of those who will receive His Son. Because of His omniscience and sovereignty, God weaves everything that happens into the overall plan and purpose for the redemption of lost mankind.

From Acts 6:8 through 9:31 we have Luke's record of how the lives of two individuals dovetailed, and the combined results of all that happened in and through them played a major role in the advancement of the cause of Christ in the first century. The martyrdom of Stephen made a profound impression on a young rabbi, Saul of Tarsus, who had zealously undertaken a personal project to decimate the new Christian movement by persecuting and imprisoning these followers of the Nazarene. Stephen, a Hellenistic Jewish believer, is described as being "full of faith and power" and one who "did great wonders and miracles among the people" (6:8). He is listed among the seven men appointed to administer the welfare work of the church (6:5). However, Stephen seemed also to have spent a great deal of time preaching to the Greek-speaking Jews. He was an excellent speaker and a powerful debater. Some of these Hellenistic Jews took it upon themselves to challenge Stephen, but they soon found that they were no match for his ready tongue. So when they found that they could not answer his arguments nor "resist the wisdom and the spirit by which he spake" (6:10), they determined to silence him. They made false accusations against him, seeking to indict him before the Sanhedrin for speaking "blasphemous words against Moses and against God" (6:11). They accused him of declaring that Jesus of Nazareth would destroy the Temple and "change the customs which Moses delivered us" (6:14). Following the accusation, Stephen made a brilliant defense of the Christian gospel before the council, beginning with Abraham and ending with the accusation that these men were not only guilty of persecuting the prophets, but they were guilty of betraying and murdering God's Messiah (7:52).

The power of the truth (vv. 54-57).—Because Stephen spoke in the power of the Spirit, those who listened were "cut to the heart, and they gnashed on him with their teeth" (7:54). They were obsessed with such rage that they gritted their teeth at Stephen.

Just at that moment, a glorious thing happened to Stephen. As he spoke his last words he looked up toward heaven and "saw the glory of God, and Jesus standing on the right hand of God" (7:55). The members of the Sanhedrin could suppress their rage no longer, and they threw their normal dignity and decorum to the wind and reacted like wild animals. Pandemonium broke loose. Any legal formalities they might have considered were cast aside and mob violence took control. They clasped their hands to their ears, implying that the words Stephen spoke were the worse kind of blasphemy, and shouted to the tops of their voices in order to drown out whatever Stephen might continue to say.

The reaction of evil (v. 58).—Even though there were attempts made to stone Jesus for blasphemy in the very courts of the Temple (John 8:59; 10:31, etc.), for some reason not given, Stephen was taken out of the city to be stoned. Those who participated in the stoning probably included the Temple guards who doubtlessly were instructed by the Sanhedrin to take Stephen out of their court to the area where he would be stoned. Then there were the Hellenistic Jews who had delivered Stephen to the Sanhedrin for trial in the first place. We can be sure that many people were thronging about to observe the outcome of this drama. As the police left the Temple area with Stephen, followed by the Sanhedrin and Stephen's accusers, people probably joined the mob along the way and followed them to the place of execution. The Sanhedrin had not legally passed a verdict to stone Stephen, and thus they were not legally liable. Thus the entire incident was the result of a violent outburst of mob violence.

According to Deuteronomy 17:6-7, the witnesses had to cast the first stones in order to attest properly that they had sworn and witnessed this prisoner's crime. Their long, loose robes had to be laid aside in order to have freedom to use their arms in the violent action of throwing stones. A young man, Saul of Tarsus, apparently was acting in some official capacity, either alone or in conjunction with others who were overseeing the stoning. Thus, from a close vantage point, Saul was able to observe Stephen. The Holy Spirit saw to it that the scene was indelibly impressed on Saul's memory.

A prayer of release (v. 59).—As stone after stone crashed against Stephen's body, he raised his face toward heaven and, after the pattern of Jesus on the cross, asked the Lord Jesus to receive his spirit. No doubt the words Jesus uttered while He was on the cross were commonly known and often rehearsed in lessons and sermons among these early Christians. Stephen did not presume to compare his martyrdom with the crucifixion of Jesus in anyway, yet it was natural for him to borrow his Lord's words at a time like this.

Stephen did not anticipate a state of oblivion at death

where the spirit is suspended in some kind of "soul sleep" until the final resurrection of the dead. Stephen had seen Jesus standing at the right hand of the Father, and he expected to be with Him shortly in full consciousness.

A prayer for his enemies (v. 60).—At the moment of Stephen's death, when his spirit actually left his body, he summoned his last ebbing strength and shouted loudly, so all in the crowd might hear, "Lord, lay not this sin to their charge." Again Stephen used words Jesus had spoken from the cross, as He, too, prayed for God's forgiveness to be granted to His persecutors. At this moment Stephen's spirit left his body, and he went to be with the Lord. When Luke stated: "he fell asleep," he referred, of course, to Stephen's physical body that would "sleep" in the grave until the resurrection. Stephen's soul, along with the souls of all the dead in Christ, will be reunited with a resurrected and glorified body.

Stephen's prayer that God would forgive his executors had at least one notable fulfillment. It was not long until Saul of Tarsus encountered the Lord Jesus Christ on the Road to Damascus, was miraculously converted, stepped into Stephen's vacant place, and carried the Christian cause forward with great power and victory.

A Prayer for a Prisoner

Acts 12:1-17

Jesus had warned His disciples that they could expect persecution from the world. He had said to them, "In the world ye shall have tribulation: but be of good cheer; I have overcome the world" (John 16:33). Sometimes that persecution resulted in martyrdom. With Acts 12, Luke returned to the Jerusalem church with his historical record and described the third major persecution that came to the believers there.

The persecution of the church (vv. 1-2).—The first persecution was instigated by the Sadducees and the chief priests who had Peter and John arrested because they were teaching the people and preaching "through Jesus the resurrection from the dead" (4:1). They were kept imprisoned overnight, and when they were brought before the Council, Peter spoke with such boldness that, in the face of the miracle of the healing of the lame man that the officials could not refute, they threatened Peter and John and released them.

The second persecution, which was much more serious, followed on the heels of Stephen's martyrdom and was spearheaded by Saul of Tarsus, who had witnessed Stephen's death. The third major persecution was even more intense, and involved Herod Agrippa I, grandson of Herod the Great. Herod Agrippa was a treacherous, superficial, extravagant character, though not as bad as his grandfather had been. He courted the favor of the Jews, especially the Pharisees, and pretended to play the role of the zealous protector of the Jewish religion. So Herod began expressing his hostility toward the Christians by abusing some of them. Soon he became bolder in his aggressive acts against Christians, resulting in the murder of James, the brother of John. Luke did not deal extensively with James' martyrdom, as he had done with the stoning of Stephen. Perhaps he gave more attention to the martyrdom of Stephen because it resulted in the dispersion of Christians in all directions, even to foreign lands (8:1-2). Still, the record of the death of James singled out an apostle of Christ and showed something of the lengths to which Herod intended to go.

The arrest of Peter (vv. 3-4).—The Jews were delighted to see Herod take such strong measures against the Christians. Of course, they were playing right into Herod's hands, for it was his purpose to gain their wholehearted approval of his rule. Thus encouraged by the response he received as a result of James's death, Herod proceeded with his campaign to harass and persecute Christians. Why Herod had Peter arrested and not any or all of the other disciples is not clear. Possibly, the disciples were absent from Jerusalem at this time, and when James returned, Herod did away with him. Then, when Peter appeared in Jerusalem, he, too, fell into Herod's hands. Apparently there was not a very long interval between these two events. It was the time of the Passover celebration, and Peter may have come to Jerusalem to spend this religious holiday time with the mother congregation.

Peter was arrested and placed under heavy guard in a prison cell which likely was located in Herod's palace. So determined was Herod that Peter not escape, he assigned four quaternions of soldiers to guard him. One set of four soldiers would do guard duty for a six-hour watch, followed by a second quaternion. Herod intended to present Peter to the people after Passover, where, no doubt, they would demand execution.

The praying church (v. 5).—News of Peter's arrest quickly reached the believers in Jerusalem. No doubt they were already in shock and grief because of the martyrdom of James. And now, so close on the heels of that tragedy, Peter, their leader and spokesman, was in prison, likely awaiting the same fate. They called a prayer meeting, and we can imagine that the meeting place in Jerusalem was filled to overflowing with believers in earnest prayer for God's intervention in Peter's situation.

Because of this relentless persecution, the believers lived in constant crisis. No one knew who would be the next victim. No doubt this time of great trouble had drawn them closer to each other and to God than they had ever been before. Their prayer certainly included a plan for Peter's release from prison and return to them, but they no doubt faced realistically the possibility that Peter might well follow James in martyrdom. So they may also have been praying that God would sustain Peter with His grace and grant him courage to bear whatever lay ahead for him.

The miracle of God's answer (vv. 6-11).—Sometimes God answers prayer in quiet, simple ways. Other times, however, His response comes in a spectacular and totally unexpected manner. Such was the case with His answer to the prayer the church prayed about Peter. While Peter slept, chained to a guard on either side so the slightest stirring of the prisoner would awake them, an angel appeared in the midst of a light that shined into Peter's cell. The chains seemed to have fallen noiselessly from Peter, and the angel told him to put on his clothing and sandals and follow him. Peter seemed as though he were in a dream and had to be told everything that he must do. The angel led Peter through the doors which apparently also opened noiselessly. They passed through two other guarded gates without being noticed, into the open court, and then to the street. The last, massive iron gate opened to let them out. Peter was free, while all of the guards were in their places with no awareness of what had happened.

The reaction of the church (vv. 12-17).—Here begins Luke's beautiful, detailed, human-interest account of this incident. In the dead of the night, Peter had made his way to Mary's house where he knew the Christians were assembled. He knocked on the door. Realizing the hostility of Herod, many of the believers probably were frightened. Who would answer the door? Surely some brave man would go! But no, it was Rhoda who went. She recognized Peter's voice at once, and in her excitement and joy, she forgot to unlock the door. She ran back to tell the good news, only to be met with disbelief from the praying believers. Peter continued to knock, and finally the believers were convinced and admitted him, no doubt overcome both with joy *and* chagrin! After he had quieted them, Peter told the whole story of his miraculous deliverance and gave orders that someone go and report to James (the leader of the Jerusalem church) and the others. Then Peter left to go "into another place" (v. 17), with his faith in prayer surely strengthened.

Application

The prayer life of a church and the attitude of its members toward prayer reveal much about the spiritual temperature and climate of a church. A church is much like an individual in that it has its own unique personality. The members of a church fellowship largely tend to develop a corporate unity in their reaction to their community, to new people, and to crises that develop in their midst. In most instances, a church absorbs the attitudes and reactions of its leadership.

Sadly, many churches place a minimal emphasis on a viable and consistent prayer life for its members. Prayer generally is treated as a perfunctory or ceremonial exercise in the public assembly. The midweek "prayer meeting," if such is even scheduled, amounts to a brief time of Bible study and perhaps listing the names of those members of the church who are ill or who have suffered some other misfortune. Prayer again is not the major focus, even though the service is called a "prayer meeting." Few churches ever call their members together to observe a day of concentrated prayer for some local or national crisis.

Every generation of Christians has encountered the normal human obstacles to effective praying. Even though the

Scriptures teach that the Holy Spirit comes to dwell within the person who receives the Lord Jesus Christ as Savior, many Christians are not consciously aware of His presence except in times of crisis. Human beings, by nature, are conditioned to that which can be seen and touched. A close friend moves away, and though contact is maintained perhaps for a while, soon time and space take their toll. Letters and phone calls become less and less frequent, and the relationship that once was warm and meaningful becomes little more than a lovely memory out of the past. Many Christians tend to react in the same way toward prayer, which is a major means of maintaining a vital relationship with God.

Christians who lived in the first century were no different. Yet conditions surrounding the young, struggling churches demanded that they maintain daily contact with God through prayer. It was a matter of survival. The three prayers we have chosen from Luke's historical record of the early church in the Book of Acts reflect the various reactions of the church to situations over which they had no control.

The first prayer had to do with the ten-day period between the ascension of Christ and the coming of the Holy Spirit on the Day of Pentecost. The element of the unknown characterized this prayer meeting, for the followers of Christ had no idea what was about to happen or even what to pray for. Sometimes we face similar periods in our lives. The situation is such that we do not know how to pray or what to ask for. During such experiences God often teaches a dual lesson—obedience and patience. In introducing one of Jesus' parables, Luke stated, "He spake a parable unto them to this end, that men ought always to pray, and not to faint" (Luke 18:1). We pray because we are exhorted to do so. Jesus had told His followers to return to Jerusalem and wait, where they engaged "in prayer and supplication"

(Acts 1:14). For ten days, nothing happened from the outside, but no doubt many things happened within and among the believers because of that concerted period of prayer.

The second prayer, the prayer Stephen prayed while he was being stoned to death because of his fearless witness for Christ, shows how the true spirit of a believer is both purified and revealed in the fires of trial and persecution. When we read of the serenity of the early Christian martyrs, we marvel at their spiritual strength and composure in the face of unbelievable torture and death. We hear today of Christians in countries where Christianity is not recognized as a true religion, and again we are astonished at their courage to face constant discrimination and persecution. Yet the evidence is that a genuine, daily relationship with God assures one of the resources to bear victoriously whatever circumstances arise in life.

The last prayer reveals both the faithfulness of the early believers to pray in times of crisis and their natural reaction of surprise when God answered their prayers. They were praying for Peter's release from prison, but they experienced difficulty in believing the news that he was free and standing outside the door seeking entrance to the house where they were praying! Christians in every generation often react to sudden and thrilling answers to prayer with momentary disbelief. Though God does not always choose to answer our prayers quickly and in accord with our request, when He does, we should hasten to recognize His gracious concern. We can be sure that the believers in Mary's house quickly shifted their praying from petition to praise.

Outline: Prayers of the Early Church

Each facet of a finely cut diamond, as it is turned toward the light, reveals the beauty and fire residing within the stone. Each recorded prayer of the early church likewise demonstrated the inner, spiritual condition of the believers. The first prayer during the ten days of waiting for the coming of the Holy Spirit fine-tuned the early Christians' obedience toward God and their patience in waiting for His answer. The second prayer prayed by Stephen on the stoning ground shows how God will give inner strength and courage at the moment of need. Finally, the intercessory prayer of the church for Peter's release from prison revealed how quickly and completely God sometimes chooses to answer our prayers. At such times we can be caught by surprise and even tempted to question the good thing that has happened.

A Prayer of Preparation: Acts 1:4,14

1. Waiting for the promise (v. 4)
2. A singleness of purpose (v. 14)
3. Faithfulness in prayer (v. 14)

A Prayer of a Martyr: Acts 7:54-60

1. The power of the truth (vv. 54-57)
2. The reaction of evil (v. 58)
3. A prayer of release (v. 59)

A Prayer for a Prisoner: Acts 12:1-17

1. The persecution of the church (vv. 1-2)
2. The arrest of Peter (vv. 3-4)
3. The praying church (v. 5)
4. The miracle of God's answer (vv. 6-11) 5. The reaction of the church (vv. 12-17)